Douglas C. Kimmel, PhD
Dawn Lundy Martin, PhD (Cand.)
Editors

D0217720

Midlife and Aging in Gay America

Midlife and Aging in Gay America has been co-published simultaneously as *Journal of Gay & Lesbian Social Services*, Volume 13, Number 4 2001.

*Pre-publication
REVIEWS,
COMMENTARIES,
EVALUATIONS . . .*

"MAGNIFICENT. This is a topic whose time has finally come. This book fills a gaping hole in the GLBT literature. . . . Each chapter is a gem. With its coverage of elder GLBTs who are vision impaired and HIV positive as well as an important chapter on GLBT retirement planning, it makes the literature human and integrated."

Mark Pope, EdD
*Associate Professor of Counseling and Family Therapy,
University of Missouri, St. Louis*

More pre-publication
REVIEWS, COMMENTARIES, EVALUATIONS . . .

"REQUIRED READING for any-one working with older popu-lations–in any setting. This book will increase awareness of a sizeable pop-ulation usually omitted from studies on aging . . . provides insight into the diverse lives of older sexual minori-ties. SEVERAL OF THE CHAPTERS, ALONE, ARE WORTH THE PRICE OF THIS BOOK. I most strongly recom-mend this book for any PSYCHOL-OGY, SOCIOLOGY, OR GERON-TOLOGY CLASS."

Helena M. Carlson, PhD
Professor Emerita of Psychology,
University of California, Santa Cruz

"A WONDERFULLY CLEAR AND INFORMATIVE over-view of the lives of older gays and lesbians in contemporary society. . . . A WEALTH OF INFORMATION. This book is important for all those concerned with aging and sexuality, including both students and profes-sionals in the field and those in-volved in social policy and delivery of services."

Bertram J. Cohler, PhD
Committee on Human Development,
University of Chicago

Midlife and Aging
in Gay America

Midlife and Aging in Gay America has been co-published simultaneously as *Journal of Gay & Lesbian Social Services*, Volume 13, Number 4 2001.

The *Journal of Gay & Lesbian Social Services* Monographic "Separates"

Below is a list of " separates," which in serials librarianship means a special issue simultaneously published as a special journal issue or double-issue *and* as a "separate" hardbound monograph. (This is a format which we also call a "DocuSerial.")

"Separates" are published because specialized libraries or professionals may wish to purchase a specific thematic issue by itself in a format which can be separately cataloged and shelved, as opposed to purchasing the journal on an on-going basis. Faculty members may also more easily consider a "separate" for classroom adoption.

"Separates" are carefully classified separately with the major book jobbers so that the journal tie-in can be noted on new book order slips to avoid duplicate purchasing.

You may wish to visit Haworth's Website at . . .

Http://www.HaworthPress.com

. . . to search our online catalog for complete tables of contents of these separates and related publications.

You may also call 1-800-HAWORTH (outside US/Canada: 607-722-5857), or Fax 1-800-895-0582 (outside US/Canada: 607-771-0012), or e-mail at:

getinfo@haworthpressinc.com

Midlife and Aging in Gay America, edited by Douglas C. Kimmel, PhD, and Dawn Lundy Martin, MA (Vol. 13, No. 4, 2001). *"MAGNIFICENT. This is a topic whose time has finally come. This book fills a gaping hole in the GLBT literature. . . . Each chapter is a gem. With its coverage of elder GLBTs who are vision impaired and HIV positive as well as an important chapter on GLBT retirement planning, it makes the literature human and integrated." (Mark Pope, EdD, Associate Professor of Counseling and Family Therapy, University of Missouri, St. Louis)*

From Hate Crimes to Human Rights: A Tribute to Matthew Shepard, edited by Mary E. Swigonski, PhD, LCSW, Robin S. Mama, PhD, and Kelly Ward, LCSW (Vol. 13, No. 1/2, 2001). *An unsparing look at prejudice and hate crimes against LGBT individuals, in such diverse areas as international law, the child welfare system, minority cultures, and LGBT relationships.*

Working-Class Gay and Bisexual Men, edited by George Alan Appleby, MSW, PhD (Vol. 12, No. 3/4, 2001). Working-Class Gay and Bisexual Men *is a powerfully persuasive work of scholarship with broad-ranging implications. Social workers, policymakers, AIDS activists, and anyone else concerned with the lives of gay and bisexual men will find this informative study an essential tool for designing effective programs.*

Gay Men and Childhood Sexual Trauma: Integrating the Shattered Self, edited by James Cassese, MSW, CSW (Vol. 12, No. 1/2, 2000). *"An excellent, thought-provoking collection of essays. Therapists who work with gay men will be grateful to have such a comprehensive resource for dealing with sexual trauma." (Rik Isensee, LCSW, Author of* Reclaiming Your Life*)*

Midlife Lesbian Relationships: Friends, Lovers, Children, and Parents, edited by Marcy R. Adelman, PhD (Vol. 11, No. 2/3, 2000). *"A careful and sensitive look at the various relationships of [lesbians at midlife] inside and outside of the therapy office. A useful addition to a growing body of literature." (Ellyn Kaschak, PhD, Professor of Psychology, San José State University, California, and Editor of the feminist quarterly journal* Women & Therapy*)*

Social Services with Transgendered Youth, edited by Gerald P. Mallon, DSW (Vol. 10, No. 3/4, 1999). *"A well-articulated book that provides valuable information about a population that has been virtually ignored. . . ." (Carol T. Tully, PhD, Associate Professor, Tulane University, School of Social Work, New Orleans, Louisiana)*

Queer Families, Common Agendas: Gay People, Lesbians, and Family Values, edited by T. Richard Sullivan, PhD (Vol. 10, No. 1, 1999). *Examines the real life experience of those affected by current laws and policies regarding homosexual families.*

Lady Boys, Tom Boys, Rent Boys: Male and Female Homosexualities in Contemporary Thailand, edited by Peter A. Jackson, PhD, and Gerard Sullivan, PhD (Vol. 9, No. 2/3, 1999). *"Brings to life issues and problems of interpreting sexual and gender identities in contemporary Thailand."* *(Nerida M. Cook, PhD, Lecturer in Sociology, Department of Sociology and Social Work, University of Tasmania, Australia)*

Working with Gay Men and Lesbians in Private Psychotherapy Practice, edited by Christopher J. Alexander, PhD (Vol. 8, No. 4, 1998). *"Rich with information that will prove especially invaluable to therapists planning to or recently having begun to work with lesbian and gay clients in private practice." (Michael Shernoff, MSW, Private Practice, NYC; Adjunct Faculty, Hunter College Graduate School of Social Work)*

Violence and Social Injustice Against Lesbian, Gay and Bisexual People, edited by Lacey M. Sloan, PhD, and Nora S. Gustavsson, PhD (Vol. 8, No. 3, 1998). *"An important and timely book that exposes the multilevel nature of violence against gay, lesbian, bisexual, and transgender people." (Dorothy Van Soest, DSW, Associate Dean, School of Social Work, University of Texas at Austin)*

The HIV-Negative Gay Man: Developing Strategies for Survival and Emotional Well-Being, edited by Steven Ball, MSW, ACSW (Vol. 8, No. 1, 1998). *"Essential reading for anyone working with HIV-negative gay men." (Walt Odets, PhD, Author, In the Shadow of the Epidemic: Being HIV-Negative in the Age of AIDS; Clinical Psychologist, private practice, Berkeley, California)*

School Experiences of Gay and Lesbian Youth: The Invisible Minority, edited by Mary B. Harris, PhD (Vol. 7, No. 4, 1998). *"Our schools are well served when authors such as these have the courage to highlight problems that schools deny and to advocate for students whom schools make invisible." (Gerald Unks, Professor, School of Education, University of North Carolina at Chapel Hill; Editor, The Gay Teen.) Provides schools with helpful suggestions for becoming places that welcome gay and lesbian students and, therefore, better serve the needs of all students.*

Rural Gays and Lesbians: Building on the Strengths of Communities, edited by James Donald Smith, ACSW, LCSW, and Ronald J. Mancoske, BSCW, DSW (Vol. 7, No. 3, 1998). *"This informative and well-written book fills a major gap in the literature and should be widely read." (James Midgley, PhD, Harry and Riva Specht Professor of Public Social Services and Dean, School of Social Welfare, University of California at Berkeley)*

Gay Widowers: Life After the Death of a Partner, edited by Michael Shernoff, MSW, ACSW (Vol. 7, No. 2, 1997). *"This inspiring book is not only for those who have experienced the tragedy of losing a partner-it's for every gay man who loves another." (Michelangelo Signorile, author, Life Outside)*

Gay and Lesbian Professionals in the Closet: Who's In, Who's Out, and Why, edited by Teresa DeCrescenzo, MSW, LCSW (Vol. 6, No. 4, 1997). *"A gripping example of the way the closet cripples us and those we try to serve." (Virginia Uribe, PhD, Founder, Project 10 Outreach to Gay and Lesbian Youth, Los Angeles Unified School District)*

Two Spirit People: American Indian Lesbian Women and Gay Men, edited by Lester B. Brown, PhD (Vol. 6, No. 2, 1997). *"A must read for educators, social workers, and other providers of social and mental health services." (Wynne DuBray, Professor, Division of Social Work, California State University)*

Social Services for Senior Gay Men and Lesbians, edited by Jean K. Quam, PhD, MSW (Vol. 6, No. 1, 1997). *"Provides a valuable overview of social service issues and practice with elder gay men and lesbians." (Outword)*

Men of Color: A Context for Service to Homosexually Active Men, edited by John F. Longres, PhD (Vol. 5, No. 2/3, 1996). *"An excellent book for the 'helping professions.' " (Feminist Bookstore News)*

Health Care for Lesbians and Gay Men: Confronting Homophobia and Heterosexism, edited by K. Jean Peterson, DSW (Vol. 5, No. 1, 1996). *"Essential reading for those concerned with the quality of health care services." (Etcetera)*

Sexual Identity on the Job: Issues and Services, edited by Alan L. Ellis, PhD, and Ellen D. B. Riggle, PhD (Vol. 4, No. 4, 1996). *"Reveals a critical need for additional research to address* *the many questions left unanswered or answered unsatisfactorily by existing research." (Sex Roles: A Journal of Research) "A key resource for addressing sexual identity concerns and issues in your workplace." (Outlines)*

Human Services for Gay People: Clinical and Community Practice, edited by Michael Shernoff, MSW, ACSW (Vol. 4, No. 2, 1996). *"This very practical book on clinical and community practice issues belongs on the shelf of every social worker, counselor, or therapist working with lesbians and gay men." (Gary A. Lloyd, PhD, ACSW, BCD, Professor and Coordinator, Institute for Research and Training in HIV/AIDS Counseling, School of Social Work, Tulane University)*

Violence in Gay and Lesbian Domestic Partnerships, edited by Claire M. Renzetti, PhD, and Charles Harvey Miley, PhD (Vol. 4, No. 1, 1996). *"A comprehensive guidebook for service providers and community and church leaders." (Small Press Magazine)*

Gays and Lesbians in Asia and the Pacific: Social and Human Services, edited by Gerard Sullivan, PhD, and Laurence Wai-Teng Leong, PhD (Vol. 3, No. 3, 1995). *"Insights in this book can provide an understanding of these cultures and provide an opportunity to better understand your own." (The Lavender Lamp)*

Lesbians of Color: Social and Human Services, edited by Hilda Hidalgo, PhD, ACSW (Vol. 3, No. 2, 1995). *"An illuminating and helpful guide for readers who wish to increase their understanding of and sensitivity toward lesbians of color and the challenges they face." (Black Caucus of the ALA Newsletter)*

Lesbian Social Services: Research Issues, edited by Carol T. Tully, PhD, MSW (Vol. 3, No. 1, 1995). *"Dr. Tully challenges us to reexamine theoretical conclusions that relate to lesbians. . . A must read." (The Lavender Lamp)*

HIV Disease: Lesbians, Gays and the Social Services, edited by Gary A. Lloyd, PhD, ACSW, and Mary Ann Kuszelewicz, MSW, ACSW (Vol. 2, No. 3/4, 1995). *"A wonderful guide to working with people with AIDS. A terrific meld of political theory and hands-on advice, it is essential, inspiring reading for anyone fighting the pandemic or assisting those living with it." (Small Press)*

Addiction and Recovery in Gay and Lesbian Persons, edited by Robert J. Kus, PhD, RN (Vol. 2, No. 1, 1995). *"Readers are well-guided through the multifaceted, sometimes confusing, and frequently challenging world of the gay or lesbian drug user." (Drug and Alcohol Review)*

Helping Gay and Lesbian Youth: New Policies, New Programs, New Practice, edited by Teresa DeCrescenzo, MSW, LCSW (Vol. 1, No. 3/4, 1994). *"Insightful and up-to-date, this handbook covers several topics relating to gay and lesbian adolescents . . . It is must reading for social workers, educators, guidance counselors, and policymakers." (Journal of Social Work Education)*

Social Services for Gay and Lesbian Couples, edited by Lawrence A. Kurdek, PhD (Vol. 1, No. 2, 1994). *"Many of the unique issues confronted by gay and lesbian couples are addressed here." (Ambush Magazine)*

Midlife and Aging in Gay America

Proceedings of the SAGE Conference 2000

Douglas C. Kimmel, PhD
Dawn Lundy Martin, PhD (Cand.)
Editors

Midlife and Aging in Gay America has been co-published simultaneously as *Journal of Gay & Lesbian Social Services*, Volume 13, Number 4 2001.

Harrington Park Press
The Haworth Social Work Practice Press
Imprints of
The Haworth Press, Inc.
New York • London • Oxford

Published by

Harrington Park Press®, 10 Alice Street, Binghamton, NY 13904-1580 USA

Harrington Park Press® is an imprint of The Haworth Press, Inc., 10 Alice Street, Binghamton, NY 13904-1580 USA.

Midlife and Aging in Gay America has been co-published simultaneously as *Journal of Gay & Lesbian Social Services*™, Volume 13, Number 4 2001.

Cover design by Jennifer M. Gaska

Library of Congress Cataloging-in-Publication Data

SAGE Conference 2000.
Midlife and aging in gay America : proceedings of the SAGE Conference 2000 / Douglas C. Kimmel, Dawn Lundy Martin, editors.
    p. cm.
"Co-published simultaneously as Journal of gay & lesbian social services, volume 13, number 4, 2001."
Includes bibliographical references and index.
    ISBN 1-56023-260-9 ((hard) : alk. paper) – ISBN1-56023-261-7 ((pbk) : alk. paper)
    1. Aged gays–United States–Congresses. 2. Middle aged gays–United States–Congresses.
I. Kimmel, Douglas C. II. Martin, Dawn Lundy. III. Senior Action in a Gay Environment (Organization) IV. Journal of gay & lesbian social services. V. Title.
HQ75.115 .S24 2000
305.244–dc21

2002003500

Indexing, Abstracting & Website/Internet Coverage

This section provides you with a list of major indexing & abstracting services. That is to say, each service began covering this periodical during the year noted in the right column. Most Websites which are listed below have indicated that they will either post, disseminate, compile, archive, cite or alert their own Website users with research-based content from this work. (This list is as current as the copyright date of this publication.)

(continued)

*Special Bibliographic Notes related to special journal issues
(separates) and indexing/abstracting:*

- indexing/abstracting services in this list will also cover material in any "separate" that is co-published simultaneously with Haworth's special thematic journal issue or DocuSerial. Indexing/abstracting usually covers material at the article/chapter level.
- monographic co-editions are intended for either non-subscribers or libraries which intend to purchase a second copy for their circulating collections.
- monographic co-editions are reported to all jobbers/wholesalers/approval plans. The source journal is listed as the "series" to assist the prevention of duplicate purchasing in the same manner utilized for books-in-series.
- to facilitate user/access services all indexing/abstracting services are encouraged to utilize the co-indexing entry note indicated at the bottom of the first page of each article/chapter/contribution.
- this is intended to assist a library user of any reference tool (whether print, electronic, online, or CD-ROM) to locate the monographic version if the library has purchased this version but not a subscription to the source journal.
- individual articles/chapters in any Haworth publication are also available through the Haworth Document Delivery Service (HDDS).

Midlife and Aging
in Gay America

CONTENTS

ABOUT THE EDITORS

Douglas C. Kimmel, PhD, is Professor Emeritus of Psychology at City College, City University of New York, where he has been on the faculty since 1970. He is author or coauthor of *Adulthood and Aging: An Interdisciplinary Developmental View; Adolescence: A Developmental Transition;* and *Psychological Perspectives on Lesbian and Gay Male Experiences.* He was a Fulbright Lecture Professor in Japan (1994-1995). He has served as chairman of the Association of Lesbian and Gay Psychologists and of APA's Committee on Gay and Lesbian Concerns. His research on older gay men began in 1976, and he was a cofounder of SAGE (Senior Action in a Gay Environment) in New York City in 1977.

Dawn Lundy Martin, MA, is a PhD student in English Literature at the University of Massachusetts at Amherst. She earned her master's degree at San Francisco State University and her BA at the University of Connecticut. Dawn coordinated the first national conference on aging in the gay and lesbian community for SAGE (Senior Action in a Gay Environment) in 1998. She is also cofounder of the Third Wave Foundation, the only organization in the United States that dedicates all of its resources toward promoting feminism among young people.

Preface

SAGE (Senior Action in a Gay Environment) is a social service agency and intergenerational group that seeks to improve the quality of life for lesbian, gay, bisexual, and transgender persons of all ages, ethnic/racial groups, and walks of life. The editors of this volume are symbolic of the intergenerational goal that is represented by SAGE. Dawn Lundy Martin is a graduate student, African-American, and was involved with SAGE as the coordinator of the first nationwide conference on lesbian, gay, bisexual, and transgender aging in 1998. Douglas C. Kimmel is a retired professor of psychology of northern European background; he was one of the co-founders of SAGE in 1977.

When SAGE began, one goal was to eliminate the myth that aging as a lesbian, gay, bisexual, or transgender person was a dreadful experience of loneliness and despair. Young people need to know that coming into the gay community can lead to a long and fulfilling life that offers great potential for creativity, friendship, love, and adventure. Everyone has the opportunity to invent their lives as they see fit, since there are no strict roles established by society. For this reason, role models such as those represented by older lesbians, gays, bisexuals, and transgenders are especially important for young and middle-aged persons to know and to emulate.

Presenters at the second nationwide conference sponsored by SAGE in New York City in May 2000 submitted the articles in this collection. Everyone was invited to send in an article or brief reports and members of the *Journal of Gay & Lesbian Social Services* editorial board reviewed these. Those that were accepted were revised and are presented here. They represent a diversity of topics and interests–a diversity almost as great as that represented by SAGE itself.

[Haworth co-indexing entry note]: "Preface." Kimmel, Douglas C., and Dawn Lundy Martin. Co-published simultaneously in *Journal of Gay & Lesbian Social Services* (Harrington Park Press, an imprint of The Haworth Press, Inc.) Vol. 13, No. 4, 2001, pp. xxiii-xxiv; and: *Midlife and Aging in Gay America* (ed: Douglas C. Kimmel, and Dawn Lundy Martin) Harrington Park Press, an imprint of The Haworth Press, Inc., 2001, pp. xiii-xiv. Single or multiple copies of this article are available for a fee from The Haworth Document Delivery Service [1-800-HAWORTH, 9:00 a.m. - 5:00 p.m. (EST). E-mail address: getinfo@haworthpressinc.com].

The book is organized into four sections. First, the keynote speeches are summarized by way of introduction to the importance of the topic for the broader society. Virginia Apuzzo is an openly lesbian, white, and a national leader in the political movement for equal rights for persons of all sexual orientations and was Assistant to President Clinton for Management and Administration; her closing speech gave the conference their "marching orders" for renewed social action on aging issues. Billy Jones is an openly gay, African-American psychiatrist, who has been prominent in the health care system of New York City; he discusses his own experience of growing older. Rose Dobrof is openly heterosexual and Jewish; she has been a member of the advisory board of SAGE since its inception and has been a national leader in the field of aging as a social worker and educator. Tina Donovan is a 61-year-old transgender woman who, in her response to the keynote speeches, gives a firsthand testimonial concerning the struggles of being transgender and getting older.

The second section is a series of three articles presenting general overviews on the issues and concerns of older lesbian, gay, and bisexual adults. Arnold Grossman and his colleagues have conducted one of the largest and most representative studies of this population to date. Lester Brown and colleagues report on four ethnographic studies of older gay men. James Kelly and Raymond Berger, pioneers in the field of gay male aging, summarize their own work.

The third section presents general topics of interest. John Yoakam discusses intergenerational relationships of older and younger gay men, recently displayed in popular films such as *Gods and Monsters.* Steven Mock reports on a study of the retirement intentions of same-sex couples. Kristina Hash describes her pilot study of caregiving experiences of older gay men and lesbians. Carol Sussman-Skalka describes vision problems and issues for older adults. Doneley Meris reports on his research among homeless HIV-infected gay men.

We thank the contributors and reviewers for helping us assemble this special volume. Raymond Berger has been especially supportive as the honorary journal editor. We hope it assists in the goal we all share in the field of aging: to have a long life that is filled with living.

Douglas C. Kimmel
Dawn Lundy Martin

Acknowledgments

As editors, we wish to gratefully acknowledge those without whom this volume would not have been possible. We first want to thank the staff of Senior Action in a Gay Environment (SAGE), especially Executive Director Terry Kaelber, for imagining a national conference on aging in the gay and lesbian community, and the conference coordinator Jeneve Brooks for making the second national conference happen. We are also indebted to Dr. Raymond Berger and the members of the editorial board of the *Journal of Gay & Lesbian Social Services* for their careful review of the manuscript.

A Call to Action

Virginia M. Apuzzo

SUMMARY. This call to action exposes how race, gender, class, and sexuality influence the plight of the aging in the United States. The author contends that in order for all people who are growing old to be able to age with equal success, aging activists with their wide range of political involvement must recognize how one's situation is complicated by overlapping social concerns–how older adults are doubly or triply discriminated against because of their sexual orientation, their race, their gender, and/or their socio-economic status. Further, activists must not fail to seize the opportunity to illuminate the concerns of older LGBT populations when LGBT-friendly elected officials are in office. In order to successfully make change, older LGBT populations first need to have a stronger presence in official data on American communities. After data are gathered, older LGBT populations will have a better chance of getting their issues

Virginia M. Apuzzo is Chair for Leadership in Public Policy at the National Gay and Lesbian Task Force's (NGLTF) Policy Institute. She is also the former Executive Director of NGLTF and, until recently, was Assistant to President Clinton for Management and Administration.

Address correspondence to: Virginia Apuzzo, 551 DeWitt Mill Road, Kingston, NY 12401.

[Haworth co-indexing entry note]: "A Call to Action." Apuzzo, Virginia M. Co-published simultaneously in *Journal of Gay & Lesbian Social Services* (Harrington Park Press, an imprint of The Haworth Press, Inc.) Vol. 13, No. 4, 2001, pp. 1-11; and: *Midlife and Aging in Gay America* (ed: Douglas C. Kimmel, and Dawn Lundy Martin) Harrington Park Press, an imprint of The Haworth Press, Inc., 2001, pp. 1-11. Single or multiple copies of this article are available for a fee from The Haworth Document Delivery Service [1-800-HAWORTH, 9:00 a.m. - 5:00 p.m. (EST). E-mail address: getinfo@haworthpressinc.com].

heard and dealt with in the official halls of American government. The LGBT community must not only look outward for change, but must engage in a self-critique of its own discriminatory practices based on age. Then, the LGBT community can begin to make real, substantive change for the older populations within it. *[Article copies available for a fee from The Haworth Document Delivery Service: 1-800-HAWORTH. E-mail address: <getinfo@haworthpressinc.com> Website: <http://www.HaworthPress.com> © 2001 by The Haworth Press, Inc. All rights reserved.]*

KEYWORDS. LGBT, older adults, government, race, gender, sexual orientation, class, activism, change

I know who you are. I would recognize you anywhere. You are the generations who have worked in the civil rights movement, organized around community health projects, worked in parishes, synagogues, and community centers in order to reach out and help others. You have been war protesters and war heroes, AIDS activists, squatters for affordable housing, and advocates for accessibility. You have signed petitions and written checks; you have addressed envelopes for one campaign or another–always swimming against a tide of cynicism, always firm in the belief that when some part of the world was broken, it was your mandate to fix it.

And here we are, fresh into a new century, looking our own aging squarely in the eye and seeing it in the cross hairs of race, ethnicity, poverty, homophobia, and transphobia. For those of us who have lived all of our lives having less access to education, working harder but earning less, living in substandard housing, and getting poorer health care, it is impossible to believe that we can all pass over that older adult line on equal footing. There are studies that prove it, but we know from experience; the impact of race, sexism, and socio-economic class on aging issues cannot be ignored.

The universe of issues related to healthy, safe, secure, and enriching lives of older persons is as broad and encompassing as life itself. What I intend to do this afternoon is select a few of the many imperatives before us and suggest that we turn this conference into an agenda for action. I am confident that the expertise and energy in this room is fully capable of enhancing and expanding on what we begin today.

We have just completed eight years of an administration that has been comparatively friendly toward the lesbian, gay, bisexual, transgender

(LGBT) community, but what have we won for LGBT elders? The answer is: very little of substance. This must never happen again. If we manage to secure from a future election cycle either a LGBT-friendly president and/or Congress, we must be prepared to put forward a federal agenda for older LGBT persons.

We should not leave this to the traditional advocacy groups for older Americans. In the past, they have failed to see beyond their heterosexism with marked consistency. Nor would I advise you to entrust this action to non-aging specific LGBT advocacy groups. With many good intentions in tow, some of these organizations are not interested in the virtually invisible LGBT aging communities. They are better prepared to deal with high profile issues than with the tedious policy work essential to changing the way the government works.

Eight years of a LGBT-friendly administration and we have no better understanding of the funding streams for social service agencies; no clearer answers to the many questions concerning the welfare of LGBT elders that we could have posed to Health and Human Services (HHS), the Social Security Administration, Housing and Urban Development; and no real commitment of participation in the White House Conference on Aging. We do not have adequate visibility in the current census. Indeed, we have no presence as a standard demographic variable in any of the dozens of research efforts from which much of our public policy will be based. Further, research apparatus in government and in academia rarely if ever ask about sexual orientation. Those that do usually are primarily concerned with sexually transmitted diseases only. We know virtually nothing about our older members, low-income members, or the numbers of same sex couples who have children or have already raised children.

This must be changed! Older LGBT populations need to have a stronger presence in official data on American communities.

The current effort on the part of the National Gay and Lesbian Task Force's (NGLTF) Policy Institute to have couples identify themselves for the census could result in us gaining some sense of the number of lesbians, gay men, bisexuals, and transgender people in domestic partnerships. But the United States Census could provide vast amounts of additional data if sexual orientation questions were structured onto the actual instrument.

One key finding of the National Institute of Health's recent Lesbian Health Study was that we know virtually nothing about lesbian health issues and that research is critically needed. Of course, we know even less about *older* lesbian health issues. Yet, access to information about these issues would not be difficult to obtain. We could easily, for instance, be incorporated into the Elder Abuse and Neglect Survey, which currently asks about a number of demographic variables, but not sexual orientation. Is isolation and neglect a significant problem for gay and lesbian seniors? We think so. And, we would be so much better prepared to secure the resources needed to address the problem if we had the data.

HHS's Administration of Aging is charged with studying the "characteristics of older people," which should certainly include we LGBTs as a distinct aging population. It should particularly focus on the issues surrounding "aging in place," rather than institutional care; this, of course, includes the ancillary issues of home health care and support services that are required to meet the quality of life issues so important for us.

I was recently at an event with a woman who, in 1978, was one of the few prominent professional women to write a check to an out lesbian candidate running for the New York State Assembly from a district in Brooklyn. I was that candidate. I recall this woman being very proud of the fact that she was able to help–in the way that someone a generation older takes pride in a dream that might well have been her own dream if times had been different.

When I met her again last year the woman seemed diminished, withdrawn, and spoke in a voice so much smaller than the one I recalled. She told me she was living in a retirement community and that she felt she had to be closeted in order to be accepted. It was the first time that I had come face to face with a problem so many of you are familiar with. All discrimination is brutal and ugly. But this struck me in a particular way. I wondered if I would ever find myself in such a terrified and lonely situation.

In *The Fountain of Age,* Betty Friedan (1993) focuses on *being at home*. She writes:

> In order to truly be at home in a place, it has to be *shared in some way* to enable us to experience our vital sense of self in human contact. It has to enable us to control our own lives, in privacy and in sharing, to feel rooted and safe leaving and returning, if we are to retain our personal identity. Though it can, and maybe must take a different shape as our needs change . . . it must [also] enable us to keep on moving and risking new adventures. (p. 12)

Those adventures should not include drive-by shootings in our neighborhoods. Nor should they be the result of having to wait endlessly to obtain Section 8 housing. Affordable, accessible, safe housing should not be something that millions in this country still aspire to have. While we are on the subject of housing, it should be noted that there are 40 states that provide no protection against discrimination in housing based on sexual orientation. And transgender people lack protections in 49 states.

ISSUES FOR THE UNITED STATES CONGRESS

The Welfare Reform Act of 1996 expanded the ability of religious institutions to provide social services–generally referred to as "charitable choice." Efforts to put more social welfare responsibility on religious institutions are before Congress. While religious institutions have a long history of providing social services, and many–particularly those in communities of color–have been at the forefront of providing vital care to the poor, it was required that the services not be provided in overtly religious environments. Also, there were mandates that federal civil rights laws requiring equal hiring practices not be violated. Charitable choice provisions eliminate both of these safeguards.

Bills currently before Congress would:

1. allow the provision of services in a house of worship and by pervasively sectarian institutions;
2. allow the display of religious art, icons, and sculptures in abundance where federally-funded services are provided; and,
3. allow religious contractors to discriminate in all aspects of employment, including a requirement that employees subscribe to the tenets of the religious faith.

These bills need to be monitored. NGLTF is part of a coalition whose efforts have thus far been effective. But, we need you to register your concern about this intersection of church and state and its potential impact on older LGBT people.

The issues of Social Security reform, Medicare, and Medicaid are also crucial areas of concern for us. They are complex but not impossible to understand. In some instances the implications of policy options for older LGBT persons are yet to be determined. But we know that they exist. It is crucial that specific policy options being considered *in each issue area* be thoroughly examined in light of the special needs of older members of our community. That means any of our organizations purporting to represent the position of the LGBT community must review these options with older representatives as part of that process. *Nothing about us without us!*

Look around this room. This room is full of people with the expertise to offer those national organizations that should be reviewing LGBT senior issues a range of information, options, and tools for change. And in support of the effort to generate the broadest understanding of what is at stake, the LGBT media should be willing to provide coverage for our work.

The Older Americans Act must be re-authored so that it includes the issues relevant to the aging LGBT community. This legislation provides funds for home and community-based services to old people. These services include congregate and home-delivered meals, adult day services, transportation, information and referral, advocacy assistance, telephone reassurance, and social, legal, and employment services. According to the National Council on Aging, the rising population of persons 65 and older has not been met with increased appropriations by Congress. In fact, rising costs have resulted in an overall *loss* of more than 40% since 1980. We need to make this Act more substantial in its commitment to *all* old people. *And,* we need to work in coalition with others to ensure that any legal definition of "family" in that legislation with include LGBT relationships.

The Health Care Assurance Act would provide assessment of individual needs on a case by case basis and give people the option of using funds that would ordinarily go to institutional care for home care services.

The issue of Medicare funding for home care has recently made the front page of *The New York Times.* Congress' 1997 effort to slow the growth of Medicare had to have been one of the shortest-sighted actions in a long time. The changes limited payments to home care agencies which provide services to people who are too sick or disabled to leave their homes. In one year the number of persons receiving home care dropped 600,000. Many went to hospitals and nursing homes (facilities whose cost far and away exceeds the cost of home care). We have no statistics on the number of older Americans who either died or went without treatment. If Congress does nothing, home health care will automatically be cut another 15% this year. This issue belongs on our agenda.

Medicare's failure to include comprehensive coverage for prescription drugs has become a national embarrassment. The need for a voluntary, affordable, comprehensive Medicare prescription drug benefit is vital. It is estimated that 25% of Medicare beneficiaries spent over $500 on prescription drugs in 1999; and 42% spent over $1000. There are several proposals currently before Congress. Each proposal raises important questions and requires careful study. We need to be a part of the process at congressional hearings, and in the dialogue that will attend each proposal's assessment. Find out where your Congressperson stands on these proposals—and why. Then, make your voice heard.

When I was a teenager, going to the doctor was a terrifying experience for me. I thought that if the examination were thorough enough, somehow the doctor would know I was a lesbian. When I had to have my appendix removed I refused, fearing that coming out of the anesthesia I would call my girlfriend's name. The result of those kinds of fears was that I stayed away from doctors for years at a time, or more specifically, until I faced a crisis.

The problems for us range from embarrassment to life-threatening neglect. Whether it is ignorance, homophobia, or transphobia, it is unacceptable. But these problems and their attendant discriminatory practices are only going to get worse as the health care system in this country deteriorates. HMOs put you in a virtual physician's lottery; you no sooner get a little confidence going to one physician when he or she or the whole HMO is gone. Then, you must contend with yet another coming out experience. The more complex your situation, the higher the stakes.

Specific sub-committees of the House of Representatives Ways and Means Committee consider the issues related to health and social security. The ranking Democrat is New York's own Representative Charles Rangel. We need to make sure that we sit down with his staff people and provide them with a clear understanding of the unique concerns we have around the issues and their effect on the older LGBT community.

ISSUES FOR THE LGBT COMMUNITY

With some of our largest, most well-funded LGBT community centers having virtually no full-time staff who deal exclusively with aging issues, and only a handful of under-funded service organizations with full-time staff committed to providing services to older members of our community, we need all the help we can get. If an LGBT organization postures as providing services to "the community" and provides no services especially for the older members of the community and targets no money for older LGBTs in its budget, how can it claim to serve "the community"? This will not be an easy issue to resolve, but if we do not start talking about this problem, it will never be addressed. This is part of what we mean when we say that older LGBT people are invisible to much of the larger gay movement.

The NGLTF Policy Institute has done an informal analysis of nine LGBT East Coast newspapers, involving over 700 pages. Only five articles included references to older LGBT people. In their general advertising sections there were no images of older persons.

In a similar informal study of five LGBT magazines (*The Advocate, MetroLife, Hero, Q.S.F.,* and *Out*) containing 542 pages, there were two articles that included some mention of older LGBT people. There were zero images of people who appeared to be in the 60s or older. While women are generally underrepresented in the LGBT press, even images of men were limited to 30-somethings. It is as if our lives are perceived to be too vacant, our issues too boring, our images too threatening.

I propose that we do to our own media what several of us did to the *New York Times* when our deaths could be found in the obituary pages, but our lives were invisible in the rest of the paper. We set up meetings with the editors, showed them the problem, offered specific suggestions, then we held them accountable. If our community publications refuse to recognize the significance of older LGBT lives, we should treat them the same way. I advise you to go through that educational process with the gay media. If there's no improvement, picket them. I can assure you, someone *will* cover *that* story! Invisibility is unacceptable. We will not be re-closeted by our own community!

Don't like the fact that LGBT folks on television are generally young, white, fashionable males? Two of the major networks have recently appointed vice presidents of diversity. Their press releases read: "As broadcasters, we believe it is our duty to reflect the public that makes up our viewing audience. We have made strides . . . but we remain eager to do what is necessary and what is right to improve that record." The networks are CBS and NBC. The third network, ABC, has had a director of diversity since 1997. These folks should know who you are and what you want to see on your television screen.

There are other ways that we can help our community. American corporations like to reinvest in the communities that they serve. If we look, for example, at Fortune 500 companies, some of them already provide non-discriminatory protection for their employees and give money to

AIDS organizations and breast cancer projects. They also make significant profits from older Americans. These are places where we might seek funding for services committed to older LGBT community members.

Here is a perfect example: Marriot is a company that employs over 133,000 people and operates over 1,800 hotel properties around the globe. Additionally, Marriot operates 113 retirement communities and a network of food distribution centers. This Fortune 500 company also supports AIDS services and men's health groups, and has a written non-discrimination policy regarding sexual orientation. What is it doing for older LGBT people? Where is its corporate giving going?

We could look at the pharmaceutical giants, too. Bristol Myers Squibb is a Fortune 500 company that provides full domestic partner health coverage and as well has a non-discrimination policy. Where does its corporate giving go? The same is true for American Home products; insurance companies (like Aetna, AllState, and The Hartford); telecommunications companies (such as Sprint and Verizon). All these companies have non-discrimination policies. All are potential contributors to organizations that support LGBT aging causes.

CREATING THE RESPONSE WE NEED

The most important lesson I learned at the White House was something I always suspected deep down inside. I have always believed that the most powerful people are not the ones locked within the White House gates, but those who stand outside. After all, is that not what the gates are all about?

Every June in cities and towns across the country we gear up to celebrate another cycle of pride. I think it is important to keep in mind that the Stonewall Rebellion was not simply an event that gave birth to a series of other events. What it began was a process–a process wherein we approached institutions that had labeled us as criminals or sick or sinners and demanded justice, fairness, and access. The constituency that dare not speak its name began to organize and speak our existence out loud. "L" words and "G" words were heard in places that made many people nervous. But we spoke slowly and helped them with pronunciation.

Like other groups that came before us, we had to learn to work a reluctant system into being a more responsive one. In many ways it was our response to the AIDS crisis that transformed us. The concerns that we raised were not simply code words for special interest items. We learned how to address matters related to the insurance and health care industries. We raised questions about the role of schools in the face of the most threatening public health crisis of our time. We insisted that the intransigence of religious institutions not be permitted to cost the lives of their members. Ours was a call aimed at the very posture of government towards its citizens. That was us. We know how to do those things.

It was not that long ago that we hid and were silent, believing in some measure that what the world said about our lives was true. Told that our lives were insignificant, we lived in a time in which lesbians and gay men were summoned to create significance. And we did. And we must continue to do so.

At a time when there are more millionaires in our country than ever before, the average income is $24,000 a year. In 1987, 32.2 million people in this country were living in poverty. By 1998, the number had risen to 38 million. According to Census Bureau statistics, the number of Americans without health insurance was 44.3 million in 1998; in addition, almost half of the nation's low-wage workers have no coverage ("Despite Booming Economy," 1999). And, of course, there is a disproportionate number of people of color in all these categories of disempowerment.

A movement for social change must recognize that these are not abstract numbers. They represent the conditions of life for real people, living in this country, today. These numbers suggest that all of problems we have been discussing here will be with us 20 years from now for yet another generation of older Americans to struggle with. It seems that despite the recent unprecedented economic boom, Americans seem to have lost confidence in what we once believed: that we could grow stronger, have health care, be secure in a social security system, take pride in a Medicare system, build schools that did not fall apart, build safe affordable housing with the same vigor that we build prisons, and create a system of government that was about people coming together to do for each other what they could not do for themselves alone. But you and I still have hope. We know that we can do something about the myriad problems that the older LGBT population faces. We have *not* given up. In fact, we are ready to fight just as we did for civil rights in 1950s and 1960s, just as we did at Stonewall.

I began by saying that I recognize the generations sitting in this audience. How you got here and what you did to make it to this moment in time is no accident, just like our capacity for greatness is no accident. We come together with an idea, an idea that together we are stronger, bigger than each of us individually. Our values and our vision will aid us. The challenges are formidable, but they do not exceed our potential–not by a long shot. We have, as an LGBT movement, posed some very fundamental questions to American society. These questions go to the heart of who we are as a people and what we really believe in. Let us never fail to be mindful of the power we have to shape these answers and sharpen our vision.

REFERENCES

Despite booming economy, number of uninsured grows. (1999, October 4). *Miami Herald*, p. A1.
Friedan, B. (1993). *The fountain of age*. New York: Simon & Schuster.

Is Having the Luck of Growing Old in the Gay, Lesbian, Bisexual, Transgender Community Good or Bad Luck?

Billy E. Jones

SUMMARY. The author considers the problems and challenges of aging for lesbian, gay, bisexual, and transgender (LGBT) elders. Ageism, loneliness, and health status are explored as major themes of aging. Loneliness and health status, in particular, are themes that often intersect differently for LGBT older persons. AIDS has left many LGBT elders with fewer friends and support networks. Among the leading health issues are depression, alcoholism, and substance abuse. *[Article copies available for a fee from The Haworth Document Delivery Service: 1-800-HAWORTH. E-mail address: <getinfo@haworthpressinc.com> Website: <http://www.HaworthPress.com> © 2001 by The Haworth Press, Inc. All rights reserved.]*

KEYWORDS. Aging, LGBT, AIDS, ageism, loneliness, health, health status

Billy E. Jones, MD, MS, became the first openly gay Commissioner in the City of New York in 1990 when he was appointed Commissioner of the NYC Department of Mental Health, Mental Retardation and Alcoholism Services. As a senior health and mental healthcare administrator with 25 years of experience in top executive positions, Dr. Jones currently serves as Senior Vice President and Medical Director of the Public Sector Division of the Magellan Behavioral Managed Care Organization.

Address correspondence to: Dr. Billy E. Jones, 56 Hamilton Terrace, New York, NY 10031.

[Haworth co-indexing entry note]: "Is Having the Luck of Growing Old in the Gay, Lesbian, Bisexual, Transgender Community Good or Bad Luck?" Jones, Billy E. Co-published simultaneously in *Journal of Gay & Lesbian Social Services* (Harrington Park Press, an imprint of The Haworth Press, Inc.) Vol. 13, No. 4, 2001, pp. 13-14; and: *Midlife and Aging in Gay America* (ed: Douglas C. Kimmel, and Dawn Lundy Martin) Harrington Park Press, an imprint of The Haworth Press, Inc., 2001, pp. 13-14. Single or multiple copies of this article are available for a fee from The Haworth Document Delivery Service [1-800-HAWORTH, 9:00 a.m. - 5:00 p.m. (EST). E-mail address: getinfo@haworthpressinc.com].

13

The problems and challenges of aging are basically the same for lesbian, gay, bisexual, and transgender elders, but there are a few added issues for the older LGBT community. In particular, the need for advanced planning for successful aging is more important.

There is a great emphasis on youth, especially in the gay male community, but it exists throughout society. Youth is highly sexualized so that the uses and appeal of it may be overly emphasized. This problem for older persons is known as ageism. *Ageism* is the internalized feeling of being less desirable, capable, important, and of being "on our way out." This is a major problem as one ages. However, the use of hormone replacement therapy (estrogen and testosterone) and Viagra to enhance sexual performance has changed the reality of some important physical changes.

Growing older also brings greater maturity, wisdom, and experience. These are benefits that come with aging. For example, we know better how to enjoy sex and to engage in sex in healthier ways than when we were young. These benefits can provide a sense of empowerment with aging as we approach an increasingly age-less society.

Loneliness is a second major theme of aging. The fear of loneliness seems to be greater than the actual reality, however. There are many interrelated factors involved. First, social institutions such as families, the church, and the legal system are less supportive of the LGBT community than they are of straight people. But important changes have occurred as a result of our hard-fought struggles. Second, AIDS has left many older gay persons with fewer friends in their support networks. This loss will be felt for generations to come. Third, intergenerational networks–the sharing of generational interests and support across generations–are more difficult in the LGBT community. Children provide this type of network, but those without children have to struggle to achieve it.

Health status is a third major theme of aging. The fear of illness and poor health is a reality for many. This leads to a concern about the sensitivity of healthcare providers to LGBT issues. Among the leading health issues are depression, alcoholism, and substance abuse. Depression not only depresses the immune system, but it also increases the effect of physical conditions such as heart disease and diabetes.

In conclusion, the luck of growing old as a gay, lesbian, bisexual, or transgender person is not necessarily either good or bad; it depends on ageism, loneliness, and health, and on the successfulness of advanced planning for one's later years. The outcome seems to be that if we can work to eliminate ageism, obtain support for dealing with loneliness, and stay in good health, the luck of growing old is good luck.

Aging in the United States Today

Rose Dobrof

SUMMARY. As the demographics of aging change in the United States, the number of persons over the age of 65 will continue to grow. By 2030, one in every five persons will be over the age of 65. Several factors are important when considering the reality of these demographic changes. First, successful aging, given new medical technologies, is more probable today than it was for our parents and grandparents. Second, the range of diverse populations within the aging communities has become recognized. Third, generational differences impact who cares for the elderly. Fourth, baby boomers, who will soon turn 65, will likely have a huge impact on society. And lastly, spiritual matters are important as we approach and enter old age. *[Article copies available for a fee from The Haworth Document Delivery Service: 1-800-HAWORTH. E-mail address: <getinfo@haworthpressinc.com> Website: <http://www.HaworthPress.com> © 2001 by The Haworth Press, Inc. All rights reserved.]*

Rose Dobrof, DSW, is Brookdale Professor of Gerontology at Hunter College of the City University of New York. In 1975 she became Founding Director of Hunter's Brookdale Center on Aging, a position she relinquished in 1994. She also served as the Co-Director, with Robert N. Butler, MD, of the Hunter College/Mount Sinai School of Medicine, Geriatric Education Center. Since 1979, Professor Dobrof has been Editor-in-Chief of the *Journal of Gerontological Social Work*. She is also a member of the Advisory Committee to SAGE.

Address correspondence to: Dr. Rose Dobrof, 104 Forster Avenue, Mount Vernon, NY 10552.

[Haworth co-indexing entry note]: "Aging in the United States Today." Dobrof, Rose. Co-published simultaneously in *Journal of Gay & Lesbian Social Services* (Harrington Park Press, an imprint of The Haworth Press, Inc.) Vol. 13, No. 4, 2001, pp. 15-17; and: *Midlife and Aging in Gay America* (ed: Douglas C. Kimmel, and Dawn Lundy Martin) Harrington Park Press, an imprint of The Haworth Press, Inc., 2001, pp. 15-17. Single or multiple copies of this article are available for a fee from The Haworth Document Delivery Service [1-800-HAWORTH, 9:00 a.m. - 5:00 p.m. (EST). E-mail address: getinfo@haworthpressinc.com].

15

KEYWORDS. Demographics, successful aging, diverse populations, generational differences, baby boomers, spirituality, gay, lesbian

The demographics of aging are changing in the United States: by 2030, one out of five persons will be over the age of 65. In colloquial parlance, it will be "Florida all over the country!" This trend will especially increase the numbers of older women and the oldest age groups, which are the fastest growing segments of the population. Let us focus on five issues that are important.

First, *successful aging* has become the expectation today. This a major change from the question that Robert Butler asked a generation ago in his historic book, *Why Survive?* Today we have improved medical care and longevity. Of course, it is still true that impairments and diseases are more prevalent among older persons than among younger persons. But we have a greater possibility of aging successfully than was the case for our parents or grandparents.

Second, the *diversity of aging* has become recognized. There are increased numbers of racial and ethnic minority elderly in the United States, as well as greater awareness that none of these groups is monolithic. There is diversity within each group. Diversity of the lesbian, gay, bisexual, and transgender aging population is also being recognized. Variation in income, medical care, health, family patterns, long-term relationships, friendship, bereavement, and loneliness are each important to consider.

Third, *generational differences* impact who cares for older people in families and in other love relationships. Families are changing in their structure and membership. However, families still provide the most care and arrange for care of their elderly members if they cannot provide it directly. Some LGBT persons are, of course, providing care to their aging parents or relatives and might benefit from community support. Some are caring for long-term partners and could benefit from groups that primarily serve the non-gay community, such as Alzheimer's support.

Fourth, the *size of the baby-boom cohort* is a major demographic change. By the year 2011, the first of the baby boom generation goes to "Golden Pond!" "Baby boomers" represent the high-birth rate cohort that was born between 1946 and 1964 who will soon reach age 65. This birth cohort has reshaped society at every stage of its life cycle–from suburbs and shopping malls to new occupational careers, housing and the impact on social security, entitlements, and Medicare programs.

Fifth, *spiritual issues* become particularly significant as the human life span continues to increase. The goal is to find meaning in daily living for the totality of our lives. We must focus on spiritual matters as we also focus on enduring into very old ages.

As the demographic makeup of the United States changes and ages, we have begun to recognize what a significant impact older people will continue to have on families, social services, and medical advances. Lesbian, gay, bisexual, and transgender older people are becoming recognized as part of the aging community who may have special needs because of their experiences within the larger society. What I have outlined is by no means exhaustive; instead, these are just some of realities that speak to the successful aging of both gay and non-gay people.

Being Transgender and Older:
A First Person Account

Tina Donovan

SUMMARY. Tina Donovan conveys her first person account of living as a transgender person and coming of age in the 1950s and 60s. She tells the story of her particularly negative experiences looking for employment and housing, and obtaining medical care. The account focuses on the implications of the lack of financial security as transgender persons who have been prohibited from attaining legitimate work began to reach old age. It also chronicles the abuses and neglect within the medical establishment as one attempts to get assistance for psychological and physical ailments. The author also shows how crucial LGBT organizations and support groups can be to transgender survival. *[Article copies available for a fee from The Haworth Document Delivery Service: 1-800-HAWORTH. E-mail address: <getinfo@haworthpressinc.com> Website: <http://www.HaworthPress.com> © 2001 by The Haworth Press, Inc. All rights reserved.]*

KEYWORDS. Transgender, aging, financial security, health care, abuse, neglect, addiction, support groups

Tina Donovan is a member of Senior Action in a Gay Environment (SAGE)/Queens. Address correspondence to: Tina Donovan, 12-20 34th Avenue, Apt. 3A, Long Island City, NY 11106.

[Haworth co-indexing entry note]: "Being Transgender and Older: A First Person Account." Donovan, Tina. Co-published simultaneously in *Journal of Gay & Lesbian Social Services* (Harrington Park Press, an imprint of The Haworth Press, Inc.) Vol. 13, No. 4, 2001, pp. 19-22; and: *Midlife and Aging in Gay America* (ed: Douglas C. Kimmel, and Dawn Lundy Martin) Harrington Park Press, an imprint of The Haworth Press, Inc., 2001, pp. 19-22. Single or multiple copies of this article are available for a fee from The Haworth Document Delivery Service [1-800-HAWORTH, 9:00 a.m. - 5:00 p.m. (EST). E-mail address: getinfo@haworthpressinc.com].

I would like to begin by telling you some things about myself. I am a woman, 61 years old and transgender. I have lived the last 27 years as a woman, much to the chagrin of my parents and some friends. They just did not understand the nature of my struggles since early childhood. I knew all along that I was female, not a male. When I revealed this information to my parents, my father said I was "nuts" and my mother cried. They both thought that my gender identification was a result of their failing to raise me in the correct way. In truth, my father was an alcoholic and very abusive to me. But, it is impossible to really know all the ways that this experience has affected my life and the lives of my brother and sister.

FIGHTING DISCRIMINATION

Being transgender, however, has had a very clear effect on my life and on my ability to find work, housing, and other forms of security. Whenever I looked for employment, though I was willing and eager, people did not usually want to employ "someone like me." Because the jobs that I could get were usually at gay bars, working as a bartender "off the books," I have nothing in my social security account, which means that when I turn 65 I will have no financial security. As a result of the discrimination that I have experienced, I have often had to depend on public assistance like welfare to allow me to survive. I was 37 years old before I had enough money to have my own place. Until then I had to sleep on the beds, couches, or floors in friends' apartments. Occasionally, I even had to sleep on streets and subways. Because it has helped me to survive for so many years, I am very concerned about the welfare reform of recent years. I believe all poor people are entitled to government aid, and it is something that our community needs to take a stand on.

But financial insecurity is not the only burden that has plagued my life. I have also suffered for many, many years with mental problems, such as depression and alcoholism. Each was a contributing factor in the continuation of the other. Coping with the medical establishment has been a living hell for me, particularly in my early years of coming to terms with my sexuality as a woman. Getting treatment, psychotherapy, especially in the form of in-patient care, was hard to find. When care did become available, whether for psychological or physical problems, there were often additional threats from healthcare workers to deal with.

One incident in particular that took place in a hospital emergency room was extremely traumatic for me. I was in the emergency room seeking treatment, which under the best of conditions is already a stressful experience. One of the nursing staff members saw on my chart the name "Thomas Donovan." The name and the face did not go together. He asked me some questions, and did not like my answers. He proceeded, in a very nasty and belittling manner, to try to lift my skirt to show the other nurses and patients that I was not what I appeared to be. He should have treated me first as a patient and as a person; my gender identity should not have been an issue for ridicule. Certainly, the nurse should have shown far more sensitivity than he did. Instead, his behavior was malicious and abusive. I was tied down and sedated. I spent two weeks under sedation before I was released. It took me a long time to get over this episode.

But, this is just one of the many negative experiences in the lives of transgender people. Another incident with a medical professional could have had a devastating effect on my long-term health. I had found a lump in my right breast and went to see my doctor. My doctor told me that "men" do not get lumps in their breasts. He refused to deal with me as a transgender person, and as a result he completely dismissed me. He told me that it was "nothing," and sent me home. Six months later, he sent me a "second" reminder that I had to come back in, despite never having sent me the first one. After that visit, they not only found one lump in my breast, they found *three.* Luckily, all the lumps were benign.

Because I am a recipient of Medicaid, every two years at the hospital I get a new doctor. I have to answer the same questions over and over again. Inevitably, the new intern goes out and gets one of his friends to come look at the "transie." They treat me as if I am some sort of freak. These types of experiences can have a negative effect on one's mental stability. In my case, they resulted in me becoming an addict. All of my stories of such abuse are not by any means conveyed here; yet these stories are indicative of the stories of others who like me are transgender and aging.

COMMUNITY ORGANIZATIONS AND THE HELP THEY OFFER

I have worried about growing older alone. I have been concerned that should I remain single, I will not have a caregiver. My experience of losing friends and lovers has shrunk my ability to make new friends and feel part of a community. However, the organizations that I belong to put me in touch with other organizations that serve different needs. As a result, my isolation has decreased and my fears about getting older alone have lessened.

As a 61-year-old woman who came up and out in the late 50s and early 60s, I think that now is the best time of my life! There are many things that I no longer have to worry about. Firstly, and most importantly, I am clean and sober and have been for over three years. It was a long and hard struggle, and if not for the help of support groups, like the ones at SAGE/Queens, I would not have made it. I love my life and who I am: a member of the LGBT community, a role model to some younger members of the community, and one who is asked to talk about her experience. I have more time to do things that I like, such as volunteering. I am in good health and I have friends. I hope that in the near future I will have a partner or a really good friend that I can share things with. I also hope that I can be of some service to the LGBT community, as well as to SAGE/Queens. This is not the end for me. It is really a beginning.

RESEARCH

Being Lesbian, Gay, Bisexual, and 60 or Older in North America

Arnold H. Grossman
Anthony R. D'Augelli
Timothy S. O'Connell

SUMMARY. This study examined mental and physical health, perceived social support, and experiences with HIV/AIDS of 416 lesbian, gay, and bisexual adults aged 60 to 91. Most participants reported fairly high levels of self-esteem; however, many experienced loneliness. Most

Arnold H. Grossman, PhD, ACSW, is Professor, Department of Health Studies, School of Education, New York University.

Anthony R. D'Augelli, PhD, is Professor, Department of Human Development and Family Studies, The Pennsylvania State University.

Timothy S. O'Connell is Doctoral Candidate, Department of Health Studies, School of Education, New York University.

Address correspondence to: Arnold H. Grossman, Department of Health Studies, School of Education, New York University, 35 West 4th Street-Suite 1200, New York, NY 10012-1172.

The authors gratefully acknowledge initial funding from NYU School of Education's Research Challenge Fund.

[Haworth co-indexing entry note]: "Being Lesbian, Gay, Bisexual, and 60 or Older in North America." Grossman, Arnold, H., Anthony R. D.'Augelli, and Timothy S. O'Connell. Co-published simultaneously in *Journal of Gay & Lesbian Social Services* (Harrington Park Press, an imprint of The Haworth Press, Inc.) Vol. 13, No. 4, 2001, pp. 23-40; and: *Midlife and Aging in Gay America* (ed: Douglas C. Kimmel, and Dawn Lundy Martin) Harrington Park Press, an imprint of The Haworth Press, Inc., 2001, pp. 23-40. Single or multiple copies of this article are available for a fee from The Haworth Document Delivery Service [1-800-HAWORTH, 9:00 a.m. - 5:00 p.m. (EST). E-mail address: getinfo@haworthpressinc.com].

also reported low levels of internalized homophobia, but men reported significantly higher levels than women did. Ten percent of respondents sometimes or often considered suicide, with men reporting significantly more suicidal thoughts related to their sexual orientation. Men also had significantly higher drinking scores than women, and more men could be classified as problem drinkers. Only 11% of the respondents said that their health status interfered with the things they wanted to do. Although 93% of the participants knew people diagnosed with HIV/AIDS, 90% said that they were unlikely to be HIV-infected. Participants averaged six people in their support networks, most of whom were close friends. Most support network members knew about the participants' sexual orientation, and the respondents were more satisfied with support from those who knew. Those living with domestic partners were less lonely and rated their physical and mental health more positively than those living alone. *[Article copies available for a fee from The Haworth Document Delivery Service: 1-800-HAWORTH. E-mail address: <getinfo@haworthpressinc.com> Website: <http://www.HaworthPress.com> © 2001 by The Haworth Press, Inc. All rights reserved.]*

KEYWORDS. Social support, homosexuality, mental health, physical health, support networks, internalized homophobia, loneliness

Most people have opinions about aging, and many people have thoughts about homosexuality. But few individuals have considered them simultaneously. In fact, many scholars, advocates for older adults, and other individuals consider the terms *gay* and *aging* to be incompatible. Consequently, there have been comparatively few studies about the lives of older lesbian, gay, and bisexual people. As a result, not only have the members of this segment of the aging population remained invisible, but myths and stereotypes have been created about them and have persisted. We decided to ask older lesbian, gay, and bisexual individuals across the country about their lives and to learn from their telling. Specifically, we designed this study to meet the following needs: (a) to give visibility to the experiences of older lesbians, gay men, and bisexual people in the gay and lesbian, aging, and academic communities; (b) to combat the myths and stereotypes about older lesbians and gay men; and (c) to expand our knowledge about older lesbians, gay men and bisexual people so as to enhance resources and programs to meet their needs.

The linking of ages to the stages of human life has been valuable in studying and learning about the experiences of various groups of people (i.e., children, adolescents, adults, and older adults). At the same time, it is important to acknowledge that there are many individual variations in developmental pathways, and the linkage of life stage and chronological age may be imprecise.

While all stages of development present challenges for all people, those individuals who are not part of society's mainstream tend to face additional hurdles. We have a growing body of knowledge proving that gay and lesbian adolescents and adults must confront additional life challenges, yet we have comparatively limited information about the lives of older lesbian, gay, and bisexual adults (see D'Augelli & Patterson, 1995; Duberman, 1997; Garnets & Kimmel, 1993; Patterson & D'Augelli, 1998; Savin-Williams & Cohen, 1996).

The study had these purposes: (a) to describe the psychosocial and health characteristics of a national sample of older lesbians, gay men, and bisexual women and men; (b) to describe the nature of the perceived support networks of older lesbians, gay men, and bisexuals; and (c) to investigate whether or not older lesbians, gay men, and bisexuals were more satisfied with the support they received from people who are aware of their sexual orientation and from people who are similar to them in terms of sexual orientation, gender, and age.

METHOD

A survey research design using a self-administered questionnaire was employed. Participants evaluated their mental emotional health, physical health, overall loneliness, responsibility for their loneliness, alcohol use, drug abuse, self-esteem, and perceived social support.

Procedures

In order to obtain a national sample for the study, we identified agencies and groups providing social, recreational, and support services to older lesbians, gay men, and bisexuals through agency networks and by community leaders. We identified a contact person for the study at each of the 19 sites (18 in the United States and one in Canada) which agreed to recruit participants. The contact person distributed and collected the study's questionnaires from those lesbians, gay men, and bisexual people 60 years and older who volunteered for the study. Each volunteer was asked to complete the questionnaire anonymously. The questionnaire was subsequently returned to the contact person in a sealed envelope. In an effort to increase the diversity of the sample, a snowball sampling approach was used. Members of the sites who agreed to participate were asked to recruit other older people who were not affiliated with their group and who were not their partners or roommates. Data collection occurred in 1997-98. Each person who completed the questionnaire was given $10.00. We report results for a final sample of 416 older lesbian, gay, and bisexual adults. A response rate cannot be calculated because the number of older adults available at each site to complete the questionnaire could not be determined.

Instrument

The questionnaire contained several standard measures and additional questions designed for this study. We assessed self-esteem using the ten-item scale developed by Rosenberg (1965); the coefficient alpha for this scale was .86 in this study. We measured internalized homophobia, or negative views of one's sexual orientation, with the Revised Homosexuality Attitude Inventory (Shidlo, 1994); the coefficient alpha was .82. We used three scales to assess dimensions of loneliness and its management. Overall loneliness was determined with an eight-item version of the UCLA Loneliness Scale (Hays & DiMatteo, 1987). The two other dimensions of loneliness–perceived responsibility for loneliness (or the attribution of the causes of loneliness to one's own efforts or to others) and the personal control over loneliness–were each assessed by four-item, four-point scales (Moore & Schultz, 1987). In this study, coefficient alphas for the three scales were .86, .86, and .57, respectively. We measured alcohol abuse with the ten-item Alcohol Use Disorders Identification Test (AUDIT), which was developed by the World Health Organization to identify people whose alcohol consumption could jeopardize their health (Bohn, Babor, & Kranzler, 1995). Coefficient alpha for the AUDIT in this study was .77. We assessed drug abuse with the ten-item version of the Drug Abuse Screening Test (DAST-10; Skinner, 1982). Coefficient alpha for the DAST-10 was .62. To measure mental and physical health, we used several questions from a survey instrument designed to assess health and mental health problems in the elderly (Ahern & Gold, 1991; Hancock Gold, Ahern, & Heller, 1991), which were answered on five-point scales. (A sample question was, "How would you describe your mental and emotional health at the present time?" answered from "Excellent" to "Very Poor.")

We used a modified version of the Support Network Survey (Berger, 1992; Berger & Mallon, 1993) to measure perceived social support. The SNS instructs the respondent to: (a) list up to 10 members of his or her support network, (b) designate the gender, age, and sexual orientation of each person and his or her relationship to the participant, (c) indicate the types of support the person gives, (d) rate his or her level of satisfaction with person's support (on a five-point scale, "not at all satisfied" to "extremely satisfied"), and (e) indicate the extent to which the person is aware of the respondent's sexual orientation (a three-item scale: 1 = "definitely knows," 2 = "definitely or probably suspects," and 3 = "does not seem to know or suspect"). The instrument also included demographic questions and items designed to assess the participants' experiences related to HIV/AIDS.

Finally, several questions concerned participants' lifelong experiences of victimization based on their sexual orientation. They were asked how often the following types of victimization had occurred: verbal insults, threats of physical violence, assaults, objects thrown, assaults with weapons, threats to have one's sexual orientation exposed, discrimination at work, and discrimination in housing. Response choices were in four categories: "never," "once," "twice," or "three or more." A total victimization score was computed by adding the scores of all types of victimization.

Participants

The sample consisted of 416 older lesbian, gay, and bisexual adults, 297 or 71% males, and 119 or 29% females. They ranged in age from 60 to 91 years, with an average age of 68.5. Most (92%) identified as lesbian or gay, and 8% identified as bisexual. More than three-fourths (79% or 327) were members of the gay-identified agencies or groups; and the remaining 21% or 89 were social contacts of those who were affiliated with the groups. About half (51%) of the respondents said they belonged to one or two gay or lesbian organizations; some reported belonging to no groups, while others reported belonging to up to 20 groups. Additionally, most participants (66%) said they regularly attended one or two groups on a regular basis. Some indicated attending no groups regularly, while others attended up to eight groups on a regular basis.

Twenty-one percent of the participants were high school graduates, 14% had obtained associate degrees or various types of certificates, and 65% received a bachelor's or higher degrees. Most participants were European/Caucasian/White, with 3% describing themselves as African-American/Black, and 2% as Hispanic/Latino or Latina. One-third (34%) lived in a major metropolitan area, while approximately another third (35%) lived in a small city; with the remainder living in a suburb (10%), a small town or rural area (13%), or another type of community (7%).

Approximately half (47% of the males and 50% of the females) stated that they had a current partner. Couples averaged 15.25 years together, with no difference between males and females in the longevity of their relationships. Almost two-thirds (63%) of the participants lived alone, 29% lived with their partners, 2% lived with friends, 2% with relatives, and 3% said they were homeless. Three-quarters (74%) were retired, 18% were working, 3% were receiving disability payments, and 5% continued to work despite retirement from other work. Participants reported being retired for an average of at least nine years ($M = 9.32$), with some participants having recently retired (three months) and others having retired over 45 years ago. With regard to personal yearly income, 15% earned less than $15,000, 44% earned from $15,000 to $35,000, and 41% earned more than $35,000.

Limitations of the Study

This study did not utilize a representative sample of older lesbian, gay, and bisexual adults. This points to the difficulty in recruiting a representative sample of older lesbian, gay, and bisexual people for health-related research. Although the sample is geographically diverse, it is biased in favor of those who participated in a gay-identified group or knew people who did. The study also used self-identification in terms of sexual identity; therefore, older adults who have had same-sex experiences but do not identify as gay, lesbian, or bisexual were not included. Consequently, the findings cannot be generalized to all older lesbian, gay, and bisexual individuals.

FINDINGS

The results of the study will be presented in five sections: mental health characteristics, selected physical health characteristics, substance use and abuse, support networks, victimization and experiences with

HIV/AIDS. Gender differences are reported as appropriate. Results for group differences on major study variables are shown in Table 1.

Mental Health Characteristics

Data were collected for six areas including overall mental health, self-esteem, loneliness, responsibility for loneliness, internalized homophobia, and suicidality.

Mental health. Eighty-four percent of the participants reported that their mental health was good to excellent, 14% said fair, and 2% poor ($M = 4.18$, $SD = .77$). Regarding changes in mental health status over the past five years, 33% said that their mental health was better currently than it was five years ago, 54% reported that it stayed the same, and 13% said it became worse ($M = 3.35$, $SD = .91$). Additionally, current mental health was significantly positively related ($r = .22$, $p < .001$) to household income, indicating those participants reporting better mental health had higher income. There was a significant negative relationship between victimization and mental health ($r = -.14$, $p < .01$), indicating those participants reporting more victimization had lower levels of mental health. There was no relationship between reported mental health and the amount of time spent with other gay men or lesbians, or with the number of gay/lesbian organizations to which participants belonged. We used analyses of variance to examine differences in reported mental health between men and women, gay men/lesbians and bisexuals, and whether or not a participant lived with a domestic partner. No differences were found between men and women, $F (1, 406) = .52$, *ns,* or between gay men/lesbians and bisexuals, $F (1, 405) = .001$, *ns.* However, those participants living with a domestic partner rated their mental health significantly more positively than whose who lived alone, $F (1, 405) = 9.13$, $p < .01$.

Self-esteem. Most of the participants reported fairly high levels of self-esteem ($M = 34.85$, $SD = 4.52$, range = 17.5-40). Those living with domestic partners ($M = 35.8$, $SD = 3.84$) reported significantly higher levels of self-esteem, $F (1, 411) = 7.78$, $p < .01$, than those living alone ($M = 34.45$, $SD = 4.74$). However, an ANOVA showed self-esteem did not differ by gender, $F (1, 413) = 1.29$, *ns,* or by sexual orientation (i.e., gay/lesbian vs. bisexual), $F (1, 409) = .25$, *ns.* Those participants with higher levels of self-esteem had greater household income ($r = .22$, $p < .001$) and more people in their support networks ($r = .15$, $p < .01$). There was also a positive relationship between self-esteem and victimization, with those with fewer instances of victimization reporting higher self-

TABLE 1. Group Differences on Major Study Variables

Variable	Gender					Sexual Orientation					Living Arrangements					Total	
	Male		Female			Gay/Lesbian		Bisexual			Alone		Domestic Partner				
	M	SD	M	SD	F	M	SD	M	SD	F	M	SD	M	SD	F	M	SD
Mental Health	4.14	.83	4.20	.75	.52	4.18	.78	4.18	.68	<.001	4.10	.83	4.36	.58	9.13**	4.18	.77
Self-Esteem	34.69	4.50	35.25	4.56	1.29	34.80	4.60	35.21	3.74	.25	34.45	4.74	35.80	3.84	7.78**	34.85	4.52
Loneliness	14.15	4.14	13.83	4.71	.46	14.07	4.35	13.84	3.92	.09	14.65	4.47	12.65	3.56	19.19***	14.06	4.31
Responsibility for Loneliness	10.47	2.63	9.79	2.73	5.58*	10.33	2.73	9.59	1.92	2.42	10.15	2.65	10.56	2.71	1.99	10.28	2.67
Internalized Homophobia	24.27	6.50	22.13	5.06	10.31**	23.40	6.23	25.98	5.46	2.42	24.29	6.49	22.14	5.21	10.44**	23.66	6.21
Suicidality	3.95	1.96	3.44	1.28	6.77**	3.80	1.84	3.79	1.41	<.001	3.84	1.81	3.71	1.82	.42	3.80	1.81
Physical Health	3.92	.79	4.00	.81	.76	3.93	.80	4.12	.74	1.75	3.88	.82	4.11	.70	7.21**	3.95	.79
Alcohol Use (AUDIT)	3.36	3.46	2.32	2.47	8.89**	3.05	3.21	3.47	3.74	.53	2.98	3.10	3.29	3.57	.78	3.71	4.37
Drug Use (DAST)	10.24	.66	10.19	.57	.52	10.24	.65	10.18	.46	.29	10.23	.64	10.24	.65	.03	10.23	.64
Victimization	4.12	4.58	2.68	3.60	8.91**	3.69	4.36	3.94	4.48	.09	3.91	4.56	3.25	3.87	1.87	3.71	4.37

*p < .05; **p < .01; ***p < .001.

esteem ($r = -.15$, $p < .01$). However, self-esteem was lower among older participants ($r = ->+"< p <.05$). As with mental health, self-esteem was not affected by spending time with other gay men or lesbians, or by involvement with gay or lesbian organizations.

Loneliness. Many participants experienced loneliness. Over one-quarter (27%) said they lacked companionship, and 13% reported feeling isolated. There was no relationship between age and loneliness, $r = .05$, *ns*. Also, the amount of time spent with other gays or lesbians and involvement in gay or lesbian organizations were not related to loneliness. There was a significant positive correlation between loneliness and household income; those reporting more income were less lonely ($r = -.18$, $p < .001$). As would be expected, participants were less lonely when they had more people in their support network ($r = -.23$, $p < .001$). There was also a significant relationship between loneliness and victimization; those who were more lonely experienced more victimization ($r = .18$, $p < .001$). An ANOVA was used to examine differences in loneliness between those living with domestic partners and those living alone; participants living with domestic partners were significantly less lonely, $F(1, 410) = 19.19$, $p < .0001$. However, the ANOVA yielded no significant differences in reported loneliness between gay men/lesbians and bisexuals, or between men and women.

Responsibility for loneliness. Slightly more than half (52%) of the respondents agreed or strongly agreed that loneliness is a person's own fault. Men ($M = 10.47$, $SD = 2.63$) were more likely to feel responsible for their loneliness, $F(1, 408) = 5.58$, $p < .05$, than women ($M = 9.79$, $SD = 2.73$). There were no differences in feeling responsible for loneliness between gay men/lesbians and bisexuals, $F(1, 405) = 2.42$, *ns,* or those living with a domestic partner and or living alone, $F(1, 407) = 1.99$, *ns.* Unlike feelings of loneliness, there was a significant positive relationship between age and responsibility for loneliness; older respondents felt more responsible for feeling lonely ($r = .15$, $p < .01$). Feeling responsible for loneliness was not related to household income, number of people in a person's support network, time spent with other gay men or lesbians, or involvement in gay and lesbian organizations.

Internalized homophobia. Most of the participants reported low levels of internalized homophobia ($M = 23.66$, $SD = 6.21$), with men ($M = 24.27$, $SD = 6.50$) reporting significantly more negative attitudes toward homosexuality than women ($M = 22.13$, $SD = 5.06$), $F(1, 411) = 10.31$, $p < .01$. Additionally, those respondents living alone reported more internalized homophobia than those living with a domestic partner, $F = (1,409) = 10.44$, $p < .01$. There was no difference in internalized homophobia between gay men/lesbians and bisexuals. Internalized homophobia was related to age; older respondents reported more homophobia ($r = .13, p < .05$). Those respondents with more household income reported less internalized homophobia ($r = -.11, p < .05$). Contact with more people appears to be related to internalized homophobia. Respondents who were members of more gay or lesbian organizations and who had greater levels of involvement in these organizations had less internalized homophobia. Additionally, those with more people in their support networks reported less internalized homophobia. Victimization was not related to internalized homophobia ($r = .04, p = ns$).

Suicidality. Related to internalized homophobia, 8% of all participants reported being depressed about their sexual orientation, and 9% had been to counseling to stop their same-sex feelings; however, 17% of all participants stated that they would prefer being heterosexual. Of all the respondents, 10% sometimes or often considered suicide. Of these, 29% said that their suicidal thoughts related to their sexual orientation, with men reporting significantly more suicidality related to their sexual orientation than women, $F(1, 406) = 6.77, p < .01$. Thirteen percent (52 people) reported a suicide attempt at some point in their lives, with most doing so between the ages of 22 and 59. We found no differences in suicidal thoughts between those who lived with a domestic partner and those living alone, $F(1, 404) = .42, ns,$ or between gay men/lesbians and bisexual people, $F(1, 402) < .001, ns$. Additionally, there were no significant relationships between suicidal thoughts and age, household income, network size, or involvement in gay or lesbian organizations.

Selected Physical Health Characteristics

Three-fourths of the participants (75%) reported that their physical health was good to excellent, 21% said fair, and 4% poor. Regarding changes in their physical health status over the past five years, 11% said that their health was better; 50% reported that it stayed the same; and, 30% said it became worse. Eleven percent described their health status as interfering with things they wanted to do. More than half (57%) indicated that they exercised regularly, 27% sometimes, 12% seldom, and only 4% never. There was no apparent difference in reported physical health between men and women, or between gay men/lesbians and bisexuals. Individuals living with a domestic partner ($M = 4.11, SD = .70$) reported significantly better physical health than those living alone ($M = 3.88, SD = .82$), $F(1,406) = 7.21, p < .01$. Physical health was related to household income; those reporting better physical health had higher incomes ($r = .24,$

$p < .001$). Additionally, individuals experiencing less lifetime victimization reported better physical health ($r = -.14, p < .01$). Although not significant, physical health status was related to the number of people in the respondents' support networks; participants who had more people in their networks reported better physical health.

Substance Use and Abuse

Only 9% of the sample (38 people) could be classified as "problem drinkers" on the AUDIT. Eleven participants added comments indicating that they were "recovering alcoholics." Men ($M = 3.36, SD = 3.46$) reported significantly more alcohol use than women ($M = 2.32, SD = 2.47$), $F (1, 412) = 8.89, p < .01$, and significantly more men could be classified as "problem drinkers." For this sample, it appears contact with other people does not affect alcohol use. There was no difference between those living with a domestic partner and those living alone, $F (1,410) = .78$, *ns*. Further, there was no relationship between alcohol use and number of people in support networks or involvement with gay or lesbian organizations, nor was alcohol use related to age. There was no relationship between alcohol use and household income, or with victimization experiences.

Eighty-three percent reported no evidence of drug abuse in the past year on the DAST, with 36 participants emphasizing abstinence from drug use by writing unsolicited comments on their questionnaires such as, "I don't do drugs," and "No drugs ever!" There were no gender differences with regard to drug abuse.

Support Networks

The 416 participants listed a total of 2,612 people in their support networks, so the respondents' networks averaged 6.3 people. Participants' sexual orientation was not related to the size of their networks. Close friends was the most frequently reported category, listed by 90% of the participants. The second most frequently reported category was partners (listed by 44%), followed by other relatives (listed by 39%), siblings (listed by 33%), and social acquaintances (listed by 32%). Co-workers were listed only by 15% of the participants, parents by 4%, and husbands/wives by 3%. Half (49%) of the people in the networks were under 60 years of age, and half were 60 or older. The range of networks members' ages was from 15 to 94 (average age = 58). Respondents were significantly older than their network members, $t [387] =$

23.56, $p < .001$, on the average by about 10 years, a finding that held for women as well as men.

Women listed significantly more people in their networks, $t [414] = 2.94$, $p < .01$, than did men, and had more women (75%) in their networks (both lesbian and heterosexual) than did men (26%). Men's networks contained more gay/bisexual males (54%) than women's networks (10%). Heterosexual men were equally represented in men's and women's networks. Bisexual women and men reported having significantly more heterosexual people in their networks compared to lesbian and gay respondents, $F (2, 390) = 6.07$, $p < .01$. An average of six people in the networks "definitely knew" the participants' sexual orientation, an average of about two persons "definitely or probably suspected," and an average of 2.5 persons "did not know or suspect." Participants were more satisfied with the support they received from those who definitely knew of their sexual orientation than from those who suspected or were unaware of it. They were most satisfied with the support provided by their lovers/partners, and they were very satisfied with the support from close friends or co-workers. An ANOVA showed significant differences among the most frequently reported category of people offering support (i.e., partners/lovers, close friends, spouse, co-workers, other relatives, and social acquaintances), $F (8, 2819) = 22.51$, $p < .0001$. Post hoc tests (Tukey Honestly Significant Difference) revealed significant ($p < .05$) differences between (a) parents and: social acquaintances, close friends, and partners/lovers; (b) siblings and: social acquaintances, close friends, and partners/lovers; (c) coworkers and: social acquaintances, close friends, and partners/lovers; and (d) other relatives and: social acquaintances, close friends, and partners/lovers. Participants were not more satisfied with the support they received from people who were of the same sexual orientation, $F (3, 2689) = 1.2$, *ns,* or who were close to them in age, $F (2, 2827) = 1.91$, *ns.* The more satisfied participants felt with support received, the less lonely they felt, $r = -.32$, $p < .01$. Regarding the types of support received, 62% indicated that they received emotional support from their networks, 54% practical support, 13% financial support, 41% advice and guidance, and 72% reported general social support (Grossman, D'Augelli, & Hershberger, 2000).

Victimization Based on Sexual Orientation

Sixty-three percent of the participants reported experiencing verbal abuse based on their sexual orientation over their lifetimes, while 29%

were victims of threats of violence, 16% experienced assault, 11% had objects thrown at them, and 12% were assaulted with a weapon. Twenty percent reported employment discrimination based on their sexual orientation, and 7% experienced housing discrimination. Being victimized by someone who threatened to disclose their sexual orientation was reported by 29% of participants. Victimization was related to gender, F (1, 398) = 8.91, $p < .01$, with men ($M = 4.12$, $SD = 4.58$) reporting more victimization than women ($M = 2.68$, $SD = 3.60$). Additionally, increased victimization was related to visibility: those participants who had memberships in more lesbian, gay, or bisexual organizations, $r = .19$, $p < .001$, or attended them regularly, $r = .16$, $p < .01$, reported more victimization. However, the size of an individual's support network was not related to victimization, $r = .007$, $p = ns$. Reported levels of victimization were related to household income; as income increased, levels of victimization decreased, $r = -.19$, $p < .001$. Although not significant, older individuals reported less victimization than their younger counterparts, $r = -.09$, $p < .10$. There was no difference in victimization reported by those individuals living with a domestic partner or those living alone, F (1,397) = 1.87, $p = ns$. Further, there was no reported difference between gay men/lesbians and bisexuals, F (1, 398) = .09, $p = ns$.

Experiences with HIV/AIDS

Ninety-three percent of the participants knew people diagnosed with HIV/AIDS, and 90% knew someone who died from HIV/AIDS. Additionally, 47% indicated they knew three or more people who had died from HIV/AIDS. Ninety percent said that are very unlikely or unlikely to be infected with HIV, 6% didn't know, 2% likely or very likely, and 2% reported being infected. Of the 2% who reported being HIV infected, eight were men and one was a woman. Participants were asked about whether or not they had been tested for HIV/AIDS, and if not, whether they planned to in the next year. Forty percent indicated they had two or more HIV/AIDS tests, 18% had only one test, and 2% expected to be tested in the next year. The remaining 40% said they did not expect to take an HIV/AIDS test.

DISCUSSION

Today's older lesbian, gay, and bisexual people grew up when heterosexism and homophobia remained largely unchallenged. Furthermore, the culture and institutions of the time reflected pathologizing models of homosexuality. Lesbians and gay men were classified as mentally ill, and they were thereby stigmatized and assigned to a low status. Therefore, in addition to the negative events related to society's homophobia, lesbians, gay men, and bisexuals experienced social stress and stigmatization as members of a sexual minority group in a dominant heterosexual society. At the center of this experience was (is) the incongruence between their culture, needs, and experiences and societal structures (DiPlacido, 1998; Meyer, 1995). This incompatibility has led lesbians, gay men, and bisexuals to experience negative life events (e.g., loss of custody of children, anti-gay violence), as well as more chronic daily hassles (e.g., hearing anti-gay jokes, always being on guard). Some studies and reports have linked minority stress to greater mental health problems, emotional distress, and depressive mood among gay men, and excessive cigarette smoking, heavy alcohol consumption, excessive weight, and high-risk sexual behaviors among lesbians and bisexual women. However, there is evidence to suggest that some gay men, lesbians, and bisexuals deal successfully with minority stress, so that it does not lead to negative health outcomes. Social support and certain personality characteristics, such as hardiness and self-esteem, have been found to moderate the negative effects of stress (DiPlacido, 1998).

The older lesbians, gays, and bisexuals in this study experienced much of their development at a time when many stress-buffering factors were not available. On the average, they were born in 1929 and were 40 years of age at the time of the 1969 Stonewall Riots in New York City, which marked the beginning of the modern lesbian, gay, bisexual, and transgender civil rights movement. They averaged 44 years of age when homosexuality was removed from the American Psychiatric Association's list of mental illnesses in 1973, 52 when the first cases of AIDS were reported in 1981, and 69 when the television character "Ellen" disclosed her sexual orientation to a national audience in 1997. Although older lesbians, gay men, and bisexuals constitute a diverse group, these life-course markers indicate that they experienced many years of stress before these sociopolitical events influenced their lives. In addition to altering the perceived status of lesbians, gay men, and bisexuals in American society, these events empowered many older people to disclose their sexual orientation for the fist time (Herdt & Beeler, 1998), and have encouraged others to attend support and social groups designed to meet their needs. As a result, the experiences resulting from these events have enabled many older lesbians and gays to construct positive identities (Friend, 1989, 1990).

The older lesbians, gay men, and bisexuals who participated in this study experienced their early identity development at time when homosexuality was synonymous with abnormality, inferiority, and shame. As a result, many feared that identifying their sexual orientation would lead to humiliation, dishonor, and rejection, so they remained invisible. They tended to internalize society's negative stereotypes about them, developing feelings of unworthiness and self-hate (Friend, 1990; Grossman, 1997). However, it appears that most of study's participants have mastered their sexual identity challenges leading to identity acceptance, identity pride, or identity synthesis (Cass, 1979), which have led them to become members of social groups of older lesbians, gay men, and bisexuals.

Their overall mastery of sexual identity development is apparent in many of the findings of the study, which is consistent with the findings of Berger (1996) and Kehoe (1989). The large majority of the participants reported fairly high levels of self-esteem, low levels of internalized homophobia, and a good or excellent mental health status. The large majority of the participants also reported no evidence of drug use in the past year, and relatively few could be classified as "problem drinkers." The large majority of the participants described support networks that consisted mainly of close friends, thereby creating "families of choice"; however, almost half (44%) also listed partners among their network members. Although the participants were most satisfied with the support that they received from partners, they were very satisfied with the support received from close friends and co-workers. The most important factor in determining support satisfaction was the knowledge of their sexual orientation by the support group member, which is a prime example of their identity acceptance and pride.

Although a majority of the participants appear to have developed some resilience to the stress related to their minority status, evidence of distress remains. Most striking is the victimization based on sexual orientation, with almost two-thirds (63%) of the participants having experienced verbal abuse, and more than a quarter (29%) threats of physical violence. A similar percentage of people (29%) reported being victimized by someone who threatened to disclose their sexual orientation to others. As indicated by Herek, Gillis, and Cogan (1999), stigma-based personal attacks on lesbian, gay, and bisexual adults are more deleterious to their mental health than other types of attacks.

The participants in this study reported other evidence of ongoing distress. For example, more than one-quarter (27%) reported feeling lonely, and more than half (52%) reported that responsibility for loneliness was a person's own fault. Other indices of continuing distress were: 10% of the participants reported sometimes or often considering suicide, 17%

feeling that they wished they were heterosexual, and increased visibility led to greater victimization experiences. If Lee's (1987) conclusion, based on his four-year longitudinal study of older gay men in Canada, is correct–i.e., successful involves being fortunate and/or skilled enough to avoid stressors (including the stress of coming out)–then these participants are engaged in such a process. Lee found that health, wealth, and lack·of loneliness were associated with high life satisfaction among the study's participants. Another distress related to their sexual orientation was knowing large numbers of people diagnosed with HIV/AIDS (93%) and who had died as a result of HIV/AIDS (93%). The impact of these experiences was not assessed, and it is recommended that future research include the implications of living as an older lesbian, gay, or bisexual person through the HIV/AIDS epidemic.

Using a snowball sampling approach, we asked older lesbian, gay, and bisexual people who belonged to social and recreational agencies and groups to tell us about themselves. There were 416 responses, producing a larger and more geographically diverse sample than has been gathered in other studies. They completed structured questionnaires to inform us about some of their experiences and current lives. We learned that our findings are consistent with a recent development in social gerontology: socioemotional selectivity theory, which posits that older adults engage in motivated processes to regulate their social interactions, with the primary purpose of controlling their emotionality (Carstensen, 1992; Carstensen, Gross, & Fung, 1998). Using this approach, the findings of the current study support the idea that older lesbian, gay, and bisexual people engage in processes to reduce the stress associated with their minority status, thereby reducing their internalized homophobia, enhancing their identity acceptance and pride, and creating supportive social networks. Future research is needed to understand these processes, not only for the implications of providing programs and services, but to help those older lesbian, gay, and bisexual people who are not able to engage in these programs and services on their own.

REFERENCES

Ahern, F. M., & Gold, C. (1991, November). *Risk due to use of alcohol and alcohol-interactive drugs among the elderly.* Paper presented at the meetings of the American Public Health Association, Atlanta.

Berger, R. M. (1992). Passing and social support among gay men. *Journal of Homosexuality, 23,* 85-97.

Berger, R. M., & Mallon, D. (1993). Social support networks of gay men. *Journal of Sociology and Social Welfare, 20*(1), 155-174.

Berger, R. M. (1996). *Gay and gray: The older homosexual man* (2nd ed.). New York: Harrington Park Press.

Bohn, M. J., Babor, T. F., & Kranzler, H. R. (1995). The Alcohol Use Disorders Identification Test (AUDIT): Validation of a screening instrument for use in medical settings. *Journal of Studies in Alcohol, 56,* 423-432.

Carstensen, L. L. (1992). Social and emotional patterns in adulthood: Support for socioemotional selectivity theory. *Psychology and Aging, 7,* 331-338.

Carstensen, L. L., Gross, J. J., & Fung, H. H. (1998). The social context of emotional experience. In K. W. Schaie & M. P. Lawton (Eds.), *Annual review of gerontology and geriatrics, Vol. 17* (pp. 325-352). New York: Springer.

Cass, V. C. (1979). Homosexual identity formation: A theoretical model. *Journal of Homosexuality, 4*(3), 219-235.

D'Augelli, A. R., & Patterson, C. J. (Eds.). (1995). *Lesbian, gay, and bisexual identities over the lifespan: Psychological perspectives.* New York: Oxford University Press.

DiPlacido, J. (1998). Minority stress among lesbians, gay men, and bisexuals: A consequence of heterosexism, homophobia, and stigmatization. In G.M. Herek (Ed.), *Stigma and sexual orientation: Understanding prejudice against lesbians, gay men, and bisexuals* (pp. 138-159). Thousand Oaks, CA: Sage.

Duberman, M. (Ed.). (1997). *A queer world: The Center for Lesbian and Gay Studies Reader.* New York: New York University Press.

Friend, R. A. (1989). Gay aging: Adjustment and the older gay male. *Alternative Lifestyles, 3,* 231-248.

Friend, R. A. (1990). Older lesbian and gay people: A theory of successful aging. *Journal of Homosexuality, 20,* 99-118.

Garnets, L. D., & Kimmel, D. C. (1993). *Psychological perspectives on lesbian and gay male experiences.* New York: Columbia University Press.

Grossman, A. H. (1997). The virtual and actual identities of older lesbians and gay men. In M. Duberman (Ed.), *A queer world: The Center for Lesbian and Gay Studies reader* (pp. 615-626). New York: New York University Press.

Grossman, A. H., D'Augelli, A. R., & Hershberger, S. L. (2000). Social support networks of lesbian, gay, and bisexual adults 60 years of age and older. *Journal of Gerontology: Psychological Sciences, 55B,* P171-P179.

Hancock Gold, C. H., Ahern, F., & Heller, D. (1991, November). *Health outcomes associated with use of alcohol and alcohol-interactive prescription drugs by the elderly.* Paper presented at the meetings of the American Gerontological Society, Boston.

Hays, R. D., & DiMatteo, M. R. (1987). A short-form measure of loneliness. *Journal of Personality Assessment, 51,* 69-81.

Herdt, G., & Beeler, J. (1998). Older gay men and lesbians in families. In C. J. Patterson & A. R. D'Augelli (Eds.), *Lesbian, gay, and bisexual identities in families: Psychological perspectives* (pp. 177-196). New York: Oxford University Press.

Herek, G. M., Gillis, J. R., & Cogan, J. C. (1999). Psychological sequelae of hate-crime victimization among lesbian, gay, and bisexual adults. *Journal of Consulting and Clinical Psychology, 67,* 945-951.

Kehoe, M. (1989). *Lesbians over sixty speak for themselves*. New York: The Haworth Press, Inc.

Lee, J. A. (1987). What can homosexual aging studies contribute to theories of aging? *Journal of Homosexuality, 13*, 43-71.

Meyer, I. H. (1995). Minority stress and mental health in gay men. *Journal of Health and Social Behavior, 36*, 38-56.

Moore, D., & Schultz, Jr., N. R. (1987). Loneliness among the elderly: The role of perceived responsibility and control. *Journal of Social Behavior and Personality, 2* (2, Pt. 2), 215-224.

Patterson, C. J., & D'Augelli, A. R. (Eds.). (1998). *Lesbian, gay, and bisexual identities in families: Psychological perspectives*. New York: Oxford University Press.

Rosenberg, M. (1965). *Society and the adolescent self-image*. Princeton, NJ: Princeton University Press.

Savin-Williams, R. C., & Cohen, K. M. (1996). *The lives of lesbians, gays, and bisexuals: Children to adults*. Fort Worth, TX: Harcourt Brace College Publishers.

Shidlo, A. (1994). Internalized homophobia: Conceptual and empirical issues in measurement. In B. Greene & G. Herek (Eds.), *Lesbian and gay psychology: Theory, research and clinical applications* (pp. 176-205). Thousand Oaks, CA: Sage.

Skinner, H. (1982). *The Drug Abuse Screening Test (DAST): Guidelines for administration and scoring*. Toronto, Canada: Addiction Research Foundation.

Gay Men: Aging Well!

Lester B. Brown
Glen R. Alley
Steven Sarosy
Gerramy Quarto
Terry Cook

SUMMARY. This report presents the findings from four ethnographic studies of older gay men (Brown, 1997; Brown, Sarosy, Cook & Quarto, 1997; Cook, 1991; Quarto, 1996; Sarosy, 1996). There were 69 total participants who ranged in age from 36 to 79 years; most were from 50 to 65 years of age. The purpose of these studies was to examine how older gay men have adjusted, psychologically and socially, to their sexual orientation and aging process. Participants reported that they spend 50% time or more with gay friends within their own age cohorts. Many reported being involved with the gay community in some capacity, while about 15% had no involvement with the gay community. Most participants were in regular contact with their families. Most stated that their families were aware of their sexual orientation. Most of the participants reported expe-

---

Lester B. Brown, PhD, is Professor in the Department of Social Work and American Indian Studies, California State University, Long Beach.

Glen R. Alley, MSW, and Steven Sarosy, MSW, are medical social workers.

Gerramy Quarto, MSW, and Terry Cook, MSW, are social workers in aging.

Address correspondence to: Lester B. Brown, Professor, Department of Social Work/American Indian Studies, California State University/Long Beach, 1250 Bellflower Boulevard, Long Beach, CA 90840.

[Haworth co-indexing entry note]: "Gay Men: Aging Well!" Brown, Lester B. et al. Co-published simultaneously in *Journal of Gay & Lesbian Social Services* (Harrington Park Press, an imprint of The Haworth Press, Inc.) Vol. 13, No. 4, 2001, pp. 41-54; and: *Midlife and Aging in Gay America* (ed: Douglas C. Kimmel, and Dawn Lundy Martin) Harrington Park Press, an imprint of The Haworth Press, Inc., 2001, pp. 41-54. Single or multiple copies of this article are available for a fee from The Haworth Document Delivery Service [1-800-HAWORTH, 9:00 a.m. - 5:00 p.m. (EST). E-mail address: getinfo@haworthpressinc.com].

41

riencing discrimination due to sexual orientation, and one third had experienced discrimination within the gay community based on age or ethnicity. With regard to sex life, the studies found an overall lowered frequency of sexual activity. Participants felt that HIV/AIDS has had a devastating impact on older gay men, interrupting the normal aging process for those who have contracted it and prematurely aging those who care for them. The studies' findings identified the qualities of healthy adaptation to aging for older gay males: having satisfying relationship, self-acceptance as one ages, good health, an active life with a variety of interests, and financial security. *[Article copies available for a fee from The Haworth Document Delivery Service: 1-800-HAWORTH. E-mail address: <getinfo@haworthpressinc.com> Website: <http://www.HaworthPress.com> © 2001 by The Haworth Press, Inc. All rights reserved.]*

KEYWORDS. Older gay men, aging process, ethnographic, discrimination, social support, community involvement, relationships, HIV/AIDS, adaptation, intergenerational

The studies (Brown, 1997; Brown, Sarosy, Cook & Quarto, 1997; Cook, 1991; Quarto, 1996; Sarosy, 1996) presented here addressed similar issues pertinent to the gay male and the aging process. The ethnographic studies were implemented over the course of five years, all between 1990 and 1995. All four studies addressed issues related to discrimination, social support and community involvement, relationship(s), HIV/AIDS, adaptation and growing older, intergenerational attitudes, and family involvement. Two studies also addressed old age and institutionalization, life accomplishments, and the participants' greatest needs.

The purpose of these studies was to examine how older gay men have adjusted, psychologically and socially, to their sexual orientation and aging process. In this paper the studies are summarized and compared to previous research. Implications for human service professionals, future research needs, and the limitations of the studies are discussed.

The study respondents were recruited mostly through convenience sampling, using a "snowball" method, which, of course, restricts the generalizability of the studies' findings. Finding respondents this way means that few, if any, of the respondents represent men who are not connected to the usual forms of social networks.

FINDINGS

The four studies had 69 participants with an age range of 36 to 79 years; most were from 50 to 65 years of age. Most of the respondents were European American but four were American Indian. Most participants were highly educated, ranging from some college and graduate degrees to post-graduate work. Incomes ranged from $20,000 a year to $70,000. Participants reported that they spend 50% time or more with gay friends within their own age cohorts.

Many reported being involved with the gay community in some capacity, while about 15% had no involvement with the gay community. Most participants in the study viewed gay bars, nightclubs, and beaches as necessary places to build camaraderie and community. They saw these places as necessary outlets for gay men to socialize and interact with other gay men. However, they also reported that they felt that these places were being utilized less by gay men in general. Although many reported going to gay bars, they also reported feeling out of place because of their ages.

Most participants were in regular contact with their families. Most stated that their families were aware of their sexual orientation. The American Indian respondents all reported their sexual orientation as being acceptable to their families and to their American Indian communities. These respondents, unlike their white counterparts, did not experience any familial problems when they came out to their families of origin. Nor did they experience any discrimination within their American Indian communities.

Most of the participants reported experiencing discrimination due to sexual orientation, and one-third had experienced discrimination within the gay community based on age or ethnicity. The American Indian respondents all commented on being treated unfairly by others in the gay community; most of this discrimination was in the context of community activities. The European American respondents experienced discrimination in the gay community because of age.

With regard to sex life, the studies found an overall lowered frequency of sexual activity. However, participants noted an increase in the quality of their sex lives. Many expressed a degree of sadness at the loss of youthful attractiveness. The loss of physical attractiveness was mentioned most often by the European American respondents as the most unfortunate aspect of aging.

Participants felt that HIV/AIDS has had a devastating impact on older gay men, interrupting the normal aging process for those who have contracted it and prematurely aging those who care for them. Several of the American Indian respondents viewed working in the area of HIV/AIDS as their way of contributing to their communities.

Participants identified four aspects of healthy adaptation to aging: strong support systems, good physical health, good finances, and having interests one likes. The worst aspects of growing older included death/loss of friends, physical deterioration, and being alone. The best aspects of growing older included the gaining of wisdom, less financial pressure, and having long-term family and friends.

With some of the participants, intergenerational attitudes among gay males were discussed. Gay men 30 years old and younger, according to the studies respondents, were reported to view gay men over 40 as wise, experienced, and learned. At the same time, other views expressed were that gay men over 40 were tired, boring, lecherous, and "over the hill."

The studies' findings identified the qualities of healthy adaptation to aging for older gay males: having a satisfying relationship, self-acceptance as one ages, good health, an active life with a variety of interests, and financial security. Participants identified the worst aspects of growing older as bodily deterioration, not recovering from illness, being disabled, not being able to care for one's self, and loss of looks and beauty.

Nearly all the respondents reported being close, somewhat close or very close to their families. Nearly all reported having active involvement within the gay community, including social, religious, and political activities.

Declining health was a concern for many of the respondents. Participants felt that there were no differences in the way straight and gay men age. However, participants identified differences based on heterosexuals being married and having children. Most of the participants reported having concealed their gay identity at crucial times in their lives for the purpose of keeping a job or avoiding discrimination. The majority of participants spent time with gay friends their own age. Many of the participants reported that their friends were their primary support system. Many of the participants were in stable relationships; a few were not. A majority believed that monogamy was an important aspect of gay male relationships.

When asked about age and institutionalization, participants feared dying in a nursing home without family and friends. All reported having lost friends, acquaintances, and loved ones to AIDS. The feelings around loss created by AIDS were substantial.

Regarding their greatest human need, most respondents indicated acceptance, validation, and love from others. Some also reported that spirituality and having a "higher power" were their greatest human needs.

LIMITATIONS

As with many studies on homosexuality, there are limitations to the research presented here. These four exploratory studies, ethnographic in method, have the limitations common to those kinds of studies. They were small in sample sizes. Most of the respondents were identified through networks of social support systems, so isolated gay men are not represented.

Participants in these studies were mostly European American (four were American Indian), Protestant, highly educated, employed, relatively affluent, and for the most part high-functioning men with considerable social support.

DISCUSSION

Like Kelly (1974, 1977), Eisdorfer et al. (1980), and Berger (1980, 1982), the studies here found that gay men continue to experience discrimination based on age or sexual orientation. Sometimes this discrimination was experienced within the gay community itself, particularly for the American Indians (Brown, 1997). Since most of the men in the four studies spent a lot of their time engaged in activities in the gay community, this is disheartening. It indicates that much more work needs to be done inside the gay community and the non-gay community to deal with the ageism and racism that gay aging men experience.

"Coming out" was an issue for all gay men. Those in these four studies almost unanimously reported being out to their families. "Passing as heterosexual," although not addressed directly in these studies, was not mentioned by the participants as a way of life. Although several mentioned "passing" at specific times with regard to a job or specific situation, most seemed to feel that others should accept them for the way they are, and they do not shy away from being openly gay. This openness appears different from the findings of Berger (1983, 1986) and Weinberg and Williams (1974). The findings about gay men hiding or not hiding their sexual orientations are interesting. Perhaps historical changes since the 1960s have finally allowed gay men to be more open with family and others. The American Indian respondents apparently did not experience any of the familial or community harshness that some of the others reported. The openness of American Indian cultures to difference is well documented (Brown, 1997). Sexual orientation is simply another form of difference for American Indian cultures.

All of the studies presented here had similar finding about their subjects' social lives. Nearly all reported spending most (at least 50%) of their social time with other gays. Their social support systems were also primary gay people. Most of the respondents reported being, or having been, in long-term relationships. Being involved in the community and being in long-term relationships increased life satisfaction, as many previous studies have shown (Berger, 1982; Lee, 1987; Weinberg & Williams, 1974). Although still concerned about age, deterioration, and potentially being alone sometime, most of the study participants reported having sturdy social supports. For the American Indian respondents this included their tribal groups as well as the larger American Indian communities.

The loss of physical attractiveness and declining physical abilities and health are perhaps the most difficult aspects of aging for gay men. Respondents mentioned these aspects in three of the present studies. These complications are not uncommon to all people who age; many may have relied on these attributes more than necessary when they were younger. In a "youth"-oriented culture such as ours, feeling this way might be expected. However, the men in the studies presented here have not allowed these complications to interfere problematically in their adjustments to aging.

For the most part, the men in these studies have integrated into the gay community, have low concern about concealing their sexual orientation, and have satisfactory sex lives: findings that fit Berger's (1980) ideas about the requirements for healthy psychological adaptation by gay men.

Perhaps the most severe impact for the people in these studies is the marked effect on HIV/AIDS on their lives. Most reported losing loved ones, friends, and acquaintances to AIDS. They reported that HIV/AIDS has disrupted the normal aging process of all they know, and that it has prematurely aged those who serve as caretakers for those with AIDS.

HIV/AIDS has obviously affected older gay men, even though they are not, as they report, as sexually active as previously. They are affected by the loss of those whom they know, as well as those whom they encounter at gay community activities. That they are so impacted indicates that more efforts might be made to provide HIV/AIDS-related activities for these older gays, who may not be at risk so much sexually as psychologically from the losses which they experience.

THEORETICAL CONSIDERATIONS

Past research has found, contrary to public opinion, that aging gay men are basically well-adjusted individuals (Berger, 1980; Kelly, 1974). The studies presented here have similar findings. In spite of the perception that aging gay men have issues that create complicated and sometimes problematic lives as they age, gay men in these studies show a resilience and an ability to deal with issues head-on and to reach what Erikson (1978) referred to as a phase of generativity as opposed to stagnation or despair. The men in these studies care for themselves, have strong social support systems, and were comfortable with their aging, even if they were dismayed (as are most adults) about declining physical attractiveness and abilities.

If one prefers the theoretical formulations of Levinson's (1978) "seasons," one may argue that the men in these studies (as well as those in previous studies) weather the stresses and crises in their adult stages. They readily examine their lives and, overall, are comfortable with where they have been, where they are, and where they are headed.

An examination or the respondents in these studies with regard to the concept of "crisis competence" (Friend, 1991; Kimmel, 1978, p. 117) reveals similar findings. For example, one of the hardest adjustments for most aging men is the loss of the spouse who has cared for them (in household terms) on a daily basis. Gay men do not have such spouses. Most gay men learned early, through challenging traditional gender roles, to care for themselves in shopping, cooking, cleaning, etc. Even though an aging gay man may lose his partner for many years, his adjustment is not necessarily burdened by having to learn such daily living skills as those just mentioned.

Gay men learning these survival skills earlier in life makes these transitions easier for them. Aging gay men have also dealt with the stress of being out and being discriminated against, ridiculed, or abandoned by those for whom they have cared, because of their sexual orientation. Having handled such stresses for years, they may be more adept at handling other stresses and crises, because they have developed many skills for just that purpose. Like heterosexual men, gay men have handled the challenges of relationships and, unlike heterosexual men, they have also dealt with the stresses of being gay, and they have learned to care for themselves. As a consequence, they are more likely than their heterosexual counterparts to be prepared overall for aging because of these developed skills. As can be seen, aging can be a significant period of empowerment for gay men.

PORTRAITS OF GAY MEN AGING WELL

The men in these studies were forthcoming about their trials and tribulations. To provide a closer look at them we are including here some portraits of aging gay men we have encountered in our work.

Jim

Jim is an 80-year-old European American man who lived in a small town in the Riverside County area of California. He was diagnosed with terminal lung cancer. He lived in a small town, which had a population approximately of 3,000 people. Jim had moved from Long Beach 15 years prior (Long Beach for the most part has a large liberal Gay and Lesbian community). However, this part of Riverside County, where Jim lived at the time of this interview, has traditionally held a staunch conservative anti-gay perspective. When interviewed, he talked about coping within such a restrictive environment. Jim reported that he only knew of one other gay couple. They lived down the street from him. But he also reported that there was a sizable population of older gay/bisexual males that would meet in public areas (parks, etc.) at night to socialize. The majority of these men lived in a nearby town, which had a large retirement community. In addition, most of these men were also married. This behavior may be explained through popular beliefs associated with the time in which these men came of age, which did not support the notion that gays or lesbians could be in an open relationship. Therefore, although they lead "straight" lives during the day, they could express themselves and meet their other affectional needs at night. According to Jim it seemed to work, and it had been going on for a long time.

Jim had a small recreational vehicle that he used to stock with liquor and soft drinks and drive it to the outskirts of town. There is an ancient Indian monument off the beaten path. Prior to the National Park Service laying claim to the property, it was a popular pick-up area for gay men. Jim reported that people would travel from as far as Palm Springs and San Francisco to enjoy the experience. He would drive there in the summer and wait for thirsty travelers and visitors to knock on his door. He reported that it was quite an angle for meeting men. He referred to his RV as his traveling "whorehouse on wheels." Jim had many stories to tell. When he died, he died satisfied with the way he lived his life.

Matthew and Tim

Matthew and Tim are a European American couple who had been together for quite some time (twenty years). Both men were in their upper 70s and had been managing within the larger community for the past 25 years. Living in the Long Beach area of California, which has a liberal reputation and sizable gay population, the two did not experience the same difficulties as Jim. However, except for a few bars within the area, there are not many places for older gay men to socialize and be accepted. As opposed to frequenting bars and other popular pick up spots, the couple preferred to remain with each other and socialize with other gay couples. Both Matthew and Tim reported that they had distant contacts with their families, but received support from friends, who were part of their cohort. Both men stated that, although they enjoyed coming of age in the bars and living the "wild life," they were interested in companionship, as well as monogamy.

After Matthew and Tim had been with each other for quite some time, Tim became ill. As mentioned above, they had distant contact with their families and relied upon each other and friends. They both reported that they received emotional and physical support from friends, whom they considered "family." These friends would assist them with grocery shopping, transportation as well as participate in their social lives. It would be impossible to differentiate between Matthew and Tim's friends and the social support system provided by the heterosexual community. One could even say that the amount of love provided rivaled families of origin.

Red

Red is a 56-year-old educator with a PhD. His first sexual experiences were at fourteen, one with a woman and one with a man. He described himself as bisexual, but most of his sexual experiences have been with men. Although Red is "out" to his family and friends, he reported that he does not choose to tell everyone in his community about his sexuality, feeling it is "none of their business." Compared to the cultural stigmatization of homosexuality among other ethnic groups, Red believes that among American Indian groups "there is no contradiction in being Indian and homosexual." Red is single presently, although he has had several long-term partners over the years. His income is about $100,000 a year. Although his health could be better, he lives comfortably and contently.

Joe

Joe is a 55-year-old educator with a PhD, who had his first sexual experience during puberty. He teaches at a university, is a tenured professor, and is active in the American Indian and gay communities. Joe lost his last two long-term partners to AIDS, although he himself is HIV-negative. Joe earns a comfortable living and presently supports two other American Indians in his home. His health is good. His advice to younger gay men is: "Make yourself known. Take pride in your accomplishments . . . . Celebrate yourself. Be a good role model."

IMPLICATIONS FOR HUMAN SERVICES

The older gay men described here and elsewhere are generally well adjusted (Kelly, 1977). They have needs similar to those of their heterosexual counterparts (Berger, 1982, 1983). The impact of AIDS on this population, including the aging process and related attitudes toward aging, is just beginning to be addressed and understood. Although this group has not historically been the majority of homosexual men with HIV/AIDS, human service providers should be aware that HIV/AIDS has definitely affected this population, including their aging process, their attitudes toward aging, and their perceptions of the generally negative stereotypes of elderly gay men.

Human service providers should be aware that older gays have the same psychological and social needs as older heterosexuals, but the stigma of homosexuality often may prevent these needs from being identified due to fear of rejection and fear of being judged. Based on the findings of these studies, older gay men face institutional barriers and discrimination.

Human service providers should be aware that the changing definition of "family" no longer exclusively applies to heterosexual orientation. For many gay people, family is comprised of close friends and supportive peers.

When making decisions regarding nursing home placement or power of attorney, human service specialists can play a supportive role by affirming and validating an older gay man, or couple, who may be fearful of having no rights or legal recourse. During bereavement human service professionals can play a crucial role providing services to the older gay client. Isolation can particularly intense for today's gay senior citizens who grew up at a time when sexual orientation was not discussed and when they were socially isolated or actively despised. Following the loss of a significant other or spouse, human service workers can assist the older gay man with bereavement counseling and appropriate grief-related therapy, when needed.

Interventions to obviate discrimination and stereotyping by others *within* the gay community are also needed. Discriminatory treatment of older gay men by other members of the gay community can be dealt with using educational efforts to decrease negative attitudes about gay aging. Much has been done to incorporate adolescent gay men into the community; much can be done to utilize those aging gay men who may feel somewhat shut out when they have so much to offer to the community as a whole.

The continued discrimination against people of color by the gay community is evident from the study reporting on American Indians. Educational efforts need to continue to decrease the segregation between the European American gay community and gay people of color.

Having a sound knowledge of community resources and social service agencies in the gay community can be of particular use when making referrals for clients. Since high levels of community integration were found in the present studies, the significance of allocating and accessing new resources to determine if they are "gay friendly" can be a crucial role for human service providers. This will not only result in meeting the needs of an older gay client but will assure the client and professional that homophobic and/or heterosexist barriers have been taken into consideration. Thus, the chance of improving the quality of life for clients will be greater.

IMPLICATIONS FOR RESEARCH

The significant impact of the HIV/AIDS epidemic on the gay male and the gay community in general is still being explored and understood. Further research can address such issues as HIV/AIDS on elderly gay men and issues related to loss and grief.

Another area for further research is that of social services for elderly gay men (Brody & Brody, 1987). There is still little information available regarding the availability and access to social services for the older gay male since the advent of the HIV/AIDS pandemic.

Personal crises and life transitions associated with aging such as retirement, relocation, bereavement, and death and dying issues need further research to determine if older gay men are coping with these events and how human service providers can address these issues in their work.

Ageism and discrimination based on sexual orientation can create special problems for the older homosexual. The majority of the research participants in these studies reported having experienced personal discrimination. Specific problems such as visiting regulations in hospitals and nursing homes, inheritance problems, and property ownership require further research.

Two obvious research needs in the study of older gay adult development are studies on persons from various cultural and racial backgrounds. Research on subgroups of gays is needed, so we will know whether all gay men are adapting psychologically and socially to the aging process. Further studies may also address the development of social service programs for older gay men and lesbians and the effectiveness of social programs and case management for older gay adults.

CONCLUSIONS

Aging gay men have the same issues about advanced age as other elderly men, but they also face unique challenges and adaptations in their daily lives. Overall, the respondents in these studies presented themselves as socially and psychologically adjusted to growing older. They live their lives as they wish. They are active in the gay community. They are sexually active. They maintain stable love relationships and social lives. That they are so well adjusted is a testament of their strength. That they may still require occasional help is normal. That we need to be aware of their lives in order to provide effective help is also clear from these studies.

The studies presented here lend strong support to previous findings that, in general, gay men adapt well to aging. All of the studies to date have found that gay men exceed their heterosexual counterparts in adjusting to aging and being prepared and able to deal with the challenges of aging. Perhaps, at this time, we can say with some conviction that gay men age significantly well and are relatively free from many of the complications experienced by their heterosexual counterparts. The studies presented here add to the body of knowledge that began with Weinberg, Williams, Kelly, and Berger, who boldly began the study of aging gay male. Those researchers and those who have followed provide convincing evidence of the normality and effective adjustment of gay men who are aging.

REFERENCES

Berger, R. (1980). Psychological adaptation of the older homosexual. *Journal of Homosexuality, 5,* 161-175.

Berger, R. (1982). *Gay and gray: The older homosexual man.* Urbana, IL: University of Illinois Press.

Berger, R. (1983). What is a homosexual? A definitional model. *Social Work, 27,* 132-35.

Berger, R. (1986). Gay men. In H. Gochros, J. Gochros, & J. Fischer (Eds.), *Helping the sexually oppressed* (pp.162-180). Englewood Cliffs, NJ: Prentice-Hall.

Brody, D., & Brody, S. J. (1987). Aged: Services. In *Encyclopedia of Social Work* (Vol. 1, pp. 106-126). Silver Springs, MD: National Association of Social Workers.

Brown, L. B. (Ed.). (1997). *Two spirit people: American Indian lesbian women and gay men.* New York: The Haworth Press, Inc.

Brown, L. B., Sarosy, S., Quarto, G., & Cook, T. (1997). *Gay men and aging.* New York: Garland.

Cook, T. C. (1991). *Homosexuality and Aging.* Unpublished Master's thesis, Department of Social Work, California State University, Long Beach.

Eisdorfer, C., Starr, B. D., Besdine, R., Birren, J., Cristafalo, V., Lawton, M., & Maddox, G. (1980). *Annual review of gerontology and geriatrics, 1,* 220-230.

Erickson, E. (1978). *Adulthood.* New York: W.W. Norton.

Friend, R.A. (1991). Older lesbian and gay people: A theory of successful aging. *Journal of Homosexuality, 20,* 99-118.

Jacobs, M. A., & Brown, L. B. (1997). American Indian lesbians and gays: An exploratory study. In L. B. Brown (Ed.). *Two spirit people: American Indian lesbian women and gay men.* New York: The Haworth Press, Inc.

Kelly, J. (1974). *Brothers and brothers: The gay man's adaptation to aging.* Unpublished doctoral dissertation, Brandeis University, Waltham, MA.

Kelly, J. (1977). The aging male homosexual: Myth and reality. *The Gerontologist, 17* (4), 328-332.

Kimmel, D. C. (1978). Adult development and aging: A gay perspective. *Journal of Social Issues, 34* (3), 113-130.

Lee, J. A. (1987). What can homosexual aging studies contribute to theories of aging? *Journal of Homosexuality, 13,* 43-71.

Levinson, D. J. (1978). *The seasons of a man's life.* New York: Alfred A. Knopf.

Quarto, J. G. (1996). *Aging in the midst of AIDS: Perspectives on the elderly gay male in the 1980s.* Unpublished Master's thesis, Department of Social Work, California State University, Long Beach.

Sarosy, S. (1996). *Pink and gray: An exploratory study on gay men and aging.* Unpublished Master's thesis, Department of Social Work, California State University, Long Beach.

Weinberg, M. S., & Williams, C. J. (1974). *Male homosexuals: Their problems and adaptations.* New York: Penguin Books.

What Are Older Gay Men Like?
An Impossible Question?

Raymond M. Berger
James J. Kelly

SUMMARY. Although the authors recognize that the question "What are older gay men like?" is impossible to answer conclusively, they endeavor to provide a better understanding of older gay men by making comparisons to the general older male population. The authors dispel a number of myths about older gay men and suggest that they adjust to the stigma of aging and achieve independence more easily than their straight counterparts. *[Article copies available for a fee from The Haworth Document Delivery Service: 1-800-HAWORTH. E-mail address: <getinfo@haworthpressinc.com> Website: <http://www.HaworthPress.com> © 2001 by The Haworth Press, Inc. All rights reserved.]*

KEYWORDS. Older gay men, older straight men, myths, stigma of aging, mastery of stigma, crisis of independence

Raymond M. Berger, PhD, is a retired professor at California State University, Long Beach. James J. Kelly, PhD, is Associate Vice-President, Extended and Continuing Education, California State University.

Address correspondence to: Dr. James J. Kelly, California State University, Hayward, 25800 Carlos Bee Boulevard, Hayward, CA 94542-3021.

[Haworth co-indexing entry note]: "What Are Older Gay Men Like? An Impossible Question?" Berger, Raymond M., and James J. Kelly. Co-published simultaneously in *Journal of Gay & Lesbian Social Services* (Harrington Park Press, an imprint of The Haworth Press, Inc.) Vol. 13, No. 4, 2001, pp. 55-64; and: *Midlife and Aging in Gay America* (ed: Douglas C. Kimmel, and Dawn Lundy Martin) Harrington Park Press, an imprint of The Haworth Press, Inc., 2001, pp. 55-64. Single or multiple copies of this article are available for a fee from The Haworth Document Delivery Service [1-800-HAWORTH, 9:00 a.m. - 5:00 p.m. (EST). E-mail address: getinfo@haworthpressinc.com].

WHAT ARE OLDER GAY MEN LIKE?

This is the question we have been asked to address at the SAGE Conference on Aging in the Lesbian, Gay, Bisexual, and Transgender Communities. But it is an impossible question.

Imagine if someone asked, "What are men like when they get older?" or "What happens to a man's sexuality as he gets older?" Or for that matter, "How do young men express their sexuality?" Most people will understand why these are impossible questions: The categories of men, young men, older men, and older gay men include so many different types of people, that any simple answer to the question would mislead.

This certainly is true for any simple answer about what older gay men are like. We have known since the time of the first Kinsey surveys (initially published in 1948), that sexual orientation cuts across every other method of grouping people: social class, race, ethnicity, nationality, and so on. We also know that as men age, they change in ways that differ for each person. In that sense, every older gay man is unique. So, is our assignment impossible? We don't think it is.

We believe it is possible to talk about older gay men in a way that will further your understanding about these men. So what we will do here is introduce you to two very different older gay men; then we'll explore the ways in which we believe older gay men are like other men in general and ways in which they are different. In the end we hope that this paper will yield a better understanding of what it means to be an older gay man.

TWO VERY DIFFERENT PORTRAITS

Peter

Peter grew up in a large and close-knit Jewish family in the New York City of the 1940s. His father owned a small wholesale bakery business and his mother was a stay-at-home parent, always there to attend to the needs of her three sons and two daughters. Peter was the oldest son and second oldest child. His parents insist that they treated Peter just the same as his siblings, and Peter agrees. His father was often absent on business. Peter recalls that he always had a close relationship with both parents, although with five children in the family, there were times when he felt "overlooked."

This was a family in which each child was encouraged to express his individuality. Although there was nothing unusual about Peter's interests as an adolescent, one particular pastime illustrates the permissive atmosphere in his family. When Peter entered junior high school he decided he wanted to be a modern dancer. Both parents supported the idea from the start, despite the fact that few boys in that era pursued this sort of interest.

But Peter's life-long interest became a desire to work with children. In high school he excelled in math and sciences, and decided that he wanted to become a pediatrician. He met his wife in medical school and together they established individual thriving practices and parented two very bright daughters.

Early in the marriage Peter realized that his most intense sexual interests were directed toward men. For many years he pursued furtive relationships with men but kept this part of his life a secret from everyone in his family. When the girls reached their teens, Peter and his wife divorced and Peter "came out" to his family. The girls chose to live with Peter, who remained a loving and involved parent, with numerous parental commitments such as membership on the local school board.

As the girls were about to enter college, Peter met Max, a free-lance writer who was a few years his junior, at a social gathering of a gay and lesbian Jewish group. Eventually they bought a home together. Max quickly became a part of the family. Today the girls are out on their own and Peter and Max look forward to their impending retirement.

Randall

Randall grew up in a small Mississippi town, the youngest of three boys, and the son of the local minister. At the age of six, Randall's father died and shortly thereafter his mother remarried. Randall remembers this event as the beginning of difficult times. His stepfather, a military man, was harsh and unloving towards his stepchildren. Randall was singled out for particularly harsh treatment because he was "different" from the other boys. From his earliest years Randall remembers wanting to play with dolls and preferring the indoor activities of girls rather than the rough and tumble of the neighborhood boys.

The summer after sixth grade, Randall's family hosted a family reunion with a large group of other children staying over at their house. One evening a group of boys went to the barn and "fooled around" with each other. This was Randall's first sexual experience. It was also to be his last for a long time. Although a number of boys were involved, only

Randall was caught and disciplined. Enraged, his stepfather sent this sensitive and delicate boy to military school where he remained until he graduated with his high school degree.

Randall emerged from this experience bitter and disillusioned. In the years that followed, he drifted from one low-paying job to another. He had a number of brief relationships with men, but they were fleeting as well. When his parents died he inherited a modest sum of money and shortly thereafter met Bill, a man who brought some stability to Randall's life. Together they renovated an old Victorian mansion, eventually turning it into a successful retirement home for the well-to-do elderly.

Randall and Bill lived and worked side by side for over twenty years. Then Randall discovered that Bill had been having secret relationships with women. This led to a fight and the eventual breakup of the couple when Bill announced that he was marrying a woman. The breakup was a terrible blow to Randall, in great part because of an impending financial loss: All the property had been placed in Bill's name, despite Randall's many years of work. In the end Randall managed to get a small sum of money out of the place which helped him to retire in Florida. He now rents a room from a friend–another older gay man. He feels lonely and unfulfilled. He regrets the difficulties he has had to face in life and wishes for more companionship.

GROWING OLDER: GAY OR STRAIGHT

What are the commonalties? How are gay men and heterosexual men alike as they age?

Someone once told me that every individual's life is like a three-legged stool. Each life is supported by three pillars–health, finances, and relationships. If the individual can keep these three supports firm as he ages, he will grow old successfully. We believe that this three-legged stool is the same for gay men and heterosexual men as they grow old. Gerontologists will agree that these are the three areas–health, finances, and companionship–that most concern older people in general, gay or straight.

Health. Will I be healthy enough to enjoy our retirement? Will I be able to travel and pursue the interests I did not have time for during our working life? In the United States many older people are also concerned about their ability to secure good medical care and health insurance coverage. (One difference between heterosexual and homosexual men, of course, is that AIDS may be a factor for the latter group. More on that below.)

Finances. Have I saved enough during our working years to continue our lifestyle after I retire? Will I have to scrimp and save just when I should be enjoying our life?

Relationships. Will I be old and lonely? Will my companion be around to share life with me?

What are the differences between older gay men and older heterosexual men?

Although the commonalties are greater than the differences, the remainder of this article with be spent on the latter because these issues are not well understood and deserve more attention than they have received. The best way to approach this task is to summarize what we know from existing empirical and clinical studies of older gay men. This article relies heavily on a survey study of 112 gay men over the age of 40 directed by senior author, Dr. Raymond M. Berger, in the late 1970s.[1]

ASKING QUESTIONS, DEBUNKING MYTHS

How Many Older Gay Men Are There?

By any measure, gay men constitute a minority group—but not a small one. By conservative estimate (assuming that 8% of the adult U.S. population is primarily homosexual), there are perhaps one million gay men in the United States over the age of forty. If you study older people, or if you provide services to them, you are sure to encounter many older gay men—even if you are not aware of their existence.

Do Older Gay Men Have Families?

In Berger's (1996) *Gay and Gray*, about one-third had married at some time in their lives, and many of these men fathered children. In recent years an increasing number of gay men have decided to become parents outside of traditional marriages. For example, a male couple might adopt children or become foster parents. This is a little studied phenomenon.

How Many Older Gay Men Are in Love Relationships?

According to Berger, two-fifths lived with a lover; about one-third currently were in an exclusive sexual relationship; over half had had an exclusive sexual relationship at some time in the past. About one-third had never had an exclusive sexual relationship with another man (1996). Compared to older heterosexual men, older gay men are less likely to live with a partner/spouse, and less likely to be exclusive in their choice of sexual partner.

What Are Two Older Homosexual Lovers Like? Does One Play the Role of Husband and One the Role of Wife?

Most older gay couples are indistinguishable from heterosexual couples. "Role-playing" is very rare.

Are Older Homosexuals With Lovers Happier Than Those Without?

It appears so. Those with lovers had higher life satisfaction, although there were no differences on other measures of psychological adjustment. From the general literature on aging, we know that older people who are married are healthier and live longer than those who are single. There is every reason to believe this is also true for older gay men who have lovers.

Where Do Older Gay Men Meet Other Gay Men?

Like their heterosexual counterparts, older gay men are to some extent "disengaged" from earlier roles and activities. Compared with younger gay men, they participate in the "public" gay community (bars, social and political clubs, etc.) less often. They rely more heavily on long-standing friendship networks. When they do seek involvement outside the home, they are more likely to participate in religious activities and social service organizations.

Do Older Gay Men Hide Their Homosexuality?

Unfortunately it is still true in most parts of the world that gay men must conceal their sexual orientation, in that they are forced to "pass" as heterosexual in many settings. This is certainly an aspect of gay aging that distinguishes it from heterosexual aging. But *Gay and Gray* (as well as other research studies) revealed some things that may be surprising. Although many people believe that older gay men are more "uptight" about revealing their gayness, the opposite was true. Compared to younger gays, older gay men worried less about "exposure." In other words, they cared less about who knows they are gay. They were also more widely known to others as gay. As gay men grow older and especially as they retire, they have less reason to "pass." They are no longer concerned about the opinions of parents and other relatives; they are less concerned about job loss and discrimination; and in general they are more secure emotionally and financially.

Are Older Gay Men Lonely?

This stereotype has been successfully pounded into the public mind by many popular films, books, plays and movies (e.g., *The Well of Loneliness, Tea and Sympathy, Boys in the Band, The Sixth Man*). The reality is that loneliness is one of the major worries of both heterosexual men and gay men, particularly as they become very old. And some studies of older gay men do show that loneliness is often a problem. But one major survey of gay men showed that older and younger gay men did not differ in self-perceived loneliness. In *Gay and Gray*, only about one-third lived alone; two-fifths lived with a lover, and the rest with roommates or family members (1996).

Are Older Gay Men Only Interested in Young Boys?

The stereotype of the older gay man as a child molester is as pernicious as it is false. The number of gay men apprehended for child molestation is no greater than their proportional representation in the population–which is to say that well over 90% of child molesters are heterosexual men.

What Kind of Sex Life Do Older Gay Men Have?

Older gay men distinguished themselves by the quality of their sex lives: Over 60% reported having sex once a week or more often, most frequently with one partner only. Three-quarters of older gay men said they were satisfied with their current sex life (Berger, 1996).

Do Older Gay Men Grow Old "Faster" Than Heterosexuals, Because of a Greater Emphasis on Youth Among Gay Men?

This "bugaboo" was often used by psychologists and others to warn younger gay men about the terrible "disadvantages" of growing older as a gay man. But in reality, there has never been any evidence for "accelerated aging." For example, gay men do not label themselves as "middle aged" and "old" any sooner than heterosexual men. And analyses of personals ads show that gay men are no more likely to request younger partners.

What Social Problems Do Older Gay Men Have?

There are certainly problems unique to older gay men. A detailed discussion is beyond the scope of this paper. But these problems include:

- Discrimination based on sexual orientation. (However, older gay men may have more in common with older heterosexual men: In *Gay and Gray* many respondents reported that they experienced age discrimination much more frequently than sexual orientation discrimination. The sexual orientation of applicants was usually unknown by employers; applicants' ages were obvious.)
- Unresponsive social services: nursing homes, funeral services, etc.
- Legal problems for male couples. (Randall, who was the focus earlier, is an example. These problems can be avoided by good legal planning.)

What About AIDS? What Effect Has It Had on Older Gay Men?

In the United States and the rest of the Western world, the AIDS epidemic has had a disproportionate effect on gay men. (The situation is different in much of the developing world.) Gay men have felt the impact in two ways. Those infected with the virus have had to face a devastating chronic illness and issues of premature mortality. In addition, until the recent development of effective drug therapies, many gay men have had to face multiple deaths of friends, colleagues, and family members. Many of those who fell ill during the 1980s were gay men in their thirties and forties. Those who survived are now in their forties, fifties, and sixties. These men face the multiple challenges of growing older and coping with chronic illness. As more effective therapies are developed, this situation may change.

A STRENGTHS PERSPECTIVE

It may surprise some to learn that there are aspects of the gay experience that may make it easier for a man to adapt to the aging process.

Here is an analogy from medicine. Traditionally, doctors advise allergic people to avoid all allergens. (Think of allergens as naturally occurring "events" that are part of living: dust, molds, foods. Even less than optimal temperatures may be allergens.) But recent medical evidence indicates that allergens–that is, challenges to our immune system–are a necessary part of our biology; they serve to "tweak" our immune systems, keeping them in optimal condition. Unchallenged and unused, our immune systems, like our muscles, will atrophy. Thus, what seemed at first to be a disadvantage, is in fact an advantage.

One might think of people who face minority experiences in a parallel way. Their experiences are, in part, a result of growing up and growing older as a member of a despised group. A lifetime of facing and overcoming the challenges ("allergens") of low self-esteem, discrimination, and oppression, strengthens rather than weakens.

How does this apply to older gay men? Included here are two factors that have been cited as helping gay men to face the challenges of growing older.

The first one may be called *mastery of stigma*. One of the great difficulties for all older people in Western cultures is that aging is stigmatized and aged people are devalued. Gay people–and no doubt members of other oppressed groups–have a unique advantage. In their adolescence and young adulthood, gay men had to learn how to manage the stigma of being gay. They had to salvage their self-esteem, for example, in the face of societal disapproval. Most gay people do this successfully. It is suggested here that when, in later life, they must face the stigma of being old, they are in a better position to adapt than their heterosexual counterparts. They have already had a successful *mastery of stigma* experience.

A similar phenomenon is what might be called *a crisis of independence*. Again, experiences early in the lives of gay men may prepare them for a more successful adaptation to old age. Heterosexual men may be less independent or self-reliant because they have always been able to rely on societal institutions. For example, it is not uncommon for many heterosexual men to go directly from the care of their family of origin to a marriage. The disadvantage of this history can be seen most clearly in the recently widowed elderly heterosexual man, who appears helpless in the face of the domestic and emotional challenges of surviving on his own. (One of the authors of this essay witnessed this in his own family when his mother was hospitalized for an illness. He was surprised to learn that his father did not know how to operate the washing machine!) This kind of dependence is almost unknown among older gay men. Even if they married, they realized full well, early in life, that they could not rely on traditional institutions to care for them. Thus, they learned to be self-reliant at an early age, a skill that then served them well in old age.

We do not mean to suggest that homosexual aging is in any way *better* than heterosexual aging. Rather, the suggestion is that we consider the unique strengths of minority groups in facing the challenges of growing older.

WRAP-UP

In this paper, we hope that we have conveyed that older gay men are like older men in general, *and* that they are also different. Of course, the data available are often more anecdotal than statistical. There is the ever-present bias inherent in recruiting primarily urban-located homosexuals, active in the gay community–usually white, well-educated, perhaps invested in denying the stigma of growing older–and not reflecting the over 65 males who, having been socialized in a repressive social climate (often rural) are less open about their sexual orientation and less prone to volunteer for studies about homosexuality in general and aging in particular. Nevertheless, the concepts presented here allow us a clearer picture of what older gay men are like. We hope future research will reveal even more.

NOTE

1. These findings are based on a study limited to the USA. (Berger, 1996). Although the information was originally published over 20 years ago, it is still representative of the best information available.

REFERENCE

Berger, R.M. (1996). *Gay and gray: The older homosexual man* (2nd ed.). New York: Harrington Park Press.

SPECIAL TOPICS

Gods or Monsters:
A Critique of Representations
in Film and Literature of Relationships
Between Older Gay Men and Younger Men

John R. Yoakam

SUMMARY. This article reviews three films, *Death in Venice, Love and Death on Long Island,* and *Gods and Monsters,* and how they depict relationships between older gay men and the younger men to whom they are attracted. The author contends that because of cultural ageism and homophobia, portrayals of intergenerational relationships between older gay men and younger men often stir negative responses. The author also reviews the scant research that exists on intergenerational gay male relationships. He points to three notable authors and one psychologist who were in long-term relationships with younger men as historical prece-

John R. Yoakam, PhD, is Assistant Professor in the Department of Social Work at the College of St. Benedict, St. Joseph, Minnesota. He serves as the chair of the Lesbian and Gay Aging Issues Network of the American Society on Aging.

Address correspondence to: John R. Yoakam, 400 Groveland Avenue #412, Minneapolis, MN 55403 (E-mail: jyoakam@csbsju.edu).

[Haworth co-indexing entry note]: "Gods or Monsters: A Critique of Representations in Film and Literature of Relationships Between Older Gay Men and Younger Men." Yoakam, John R. Co-published simultaneously in *Journal of Gay & Lesbian Social Services* (Harrington Park Press, an imprint of The Haworth Press, Inc.) Vol. 13, No. 4, 2001, pp. 65-80; and: *Midlife and Aging in Gay America* (ed: Douglas C. Kimmel, and Dawn Lundy Martin) Harrington Park Press, an imprint of The Haworth Press, Inc., 2001, pp. 65-80. Single or multiple copies of this article are available for a fee from The Haworth Document Delivery Service [1-800-HAWORTH, 9:00 a.m. - 5:00 p.m. (EST). E-mail address: getinfo@haworthpressinc.com].

dents. He presents vignettes of five contemporary gay male relationships where there is a twelve to thirty-four year age differences to illustrate the value, importance, and challenges for these men. *[Article copies available for a fee from The Haworth Document Delivery Service: 1-800-HAWORTH. E-mail address: <getinfo@haworthpressinc.com> Website: <http://www.HaworthPress. com> © 2001 by The Haworth Press, Inc. All rights reserved.]*

KEYWORDS. Intergenerational relationships, older gay men, younger men, film, literature, ageism, homophobia, long-term relationships

When I was twenty-four years old I traveled to Ireland with my then boyfriend, Allan, who was thirty-six years old. The following Christmas I came out to my family. Although my parents were surprised to learn that I was gay, my sister had suspected. She recalled seeing the photograph of Allan and me near a ruined abbey in Ireland. Our age difference stirred her suspicion; she wondered why I would be traveling with an older man. What was the nature of our relationship?

A few years later a friend of mine in his forties was traveling in Hawaii with a boyfriend who was about fifteen years younger. My friend, Bob, commented that he and his boyfriend were treated well by the Hawaiians. However, the tourists from the mainland pointed their fingers and made negative comments about them. He concluded that the differences in their ages probably alerted them to the fact that they were a gay couple, a relationship that the onlookers disapproved of both for being homosexual as well as intergenerational.

It is my contention that when one sees an intergenerational male relationship it can stir up a powerful mixture of homophobia and ageism in a culture that assumes heterosexuality as the norm and regards intergenerational sexual relationships, be they homosexual or heterosexual, as inappropriate and exploitative.

In such relationships the elder is believed to be love starved and eager to recapture lost youth while the younger is portrayed as exploitative of the older partner's wealth and status. I have selected three films that illustrate this hypothesis: *Death in Venice* (1971), *Love and Death on Long Island* (1996), and *Gods and Monsters* (1998). All three films depict middle-aged or older men who have an erotic attraction for younger men, whose sexual orientations are either unknown or assumed to be heterosexual.

To be fair, Hollywood does not offer many films where heterosexual intergenerational relationships are portrayed positively either. For example, *Sunset Boulevard* (1950) portrays the faded silent film star, Norma Desmond, who has trapped a screenwriter, Joe Gillis, into an economically dependent relationship. She shoots him when he attempts to leave her. *Harold and Maude* (1970) playfully depicts a confused young man about to be drafted into the military who develops a friendship with a mischievous old woman. In the end, Maude commits suicide by taking pills on her 80th birthday, a plan she presumably hatched prior to meeting the young Harold. Just as in gay- and lesbian-themed films, characters involved in intergenerational relationship in heterosexual films often come to a tragic end.

I viewed *Death in Venice* in 1971, the first year I was exploring the gay world. The film, by Luchino Visconti, is based on the novella, *Tod in Venedig,* by Thomas Mann. It is brilliantly shot on location in Venice and set at the turn of the twentieth century. The main character, Aschenbach, a German writer in the book and composer in the film, has traveled to Venice for a rest cure. When he arrives at his hotel, he notices a fourteen-year-old Polish lad named Tadzio, who is on holiday with his family. Aschenbach is so enamored of Tadzio that he can't keep his eyes off of him. He stares at him at the beach. He follows Tadzio and his family on their sojourns into the city and to church. As the story progresses, the beach hotel where Aschenbach is staying slowly empties out. Warnings are posted about infection control. Aschenbach receives a tip that cholera is moving from the east up the Mediterranean to Venice, which will soon be quarantined. In a moment of despair Aschenbach goes to a barber who persuades the aging composer to dye his hair. The barber also daubs the composer's face with powder, rubs his cheeks with rouge, and colors his lips with lipstick. Aschenbach returns to the beach to look at Tadzio once more before the lad and his family return to Poland. Aschenbach catches one last endlessly enduring glance at Tadzio, who points out to the sea. Aschenbach rises from his chair, suddenly collapses, suffers a heart attack, and dies, without ever consummating so much as a conversation or a physical touch with the young man.

Stuart Byron, who reviewed the film for the *Village Voice* in July of 1971, reacted to other reviewers who complained of the film's reducing Mann's novel to "mere homosexuality." Byron believed that the greatness of Mann's story, however, lay in its ambivalence . . . about ideas of sensuality which go beyond physical sex. Yet, in the film Aschenbach succumbs to the barber's direction to transform him into a seemingly more attractive physical object in order to appear more youthful to Tadzio. The dye from Aschenbach's hair runs down his distraught, powdered face as he stares longingly at the beautiful Tadzio for the final time before death. Byron concluded that *Death in Venice* was unquestionably "the finest movie on gay oppression and liberation to date." Given that there were few films depicting gay men prior to 1971, there was obviously not much of a field within which to compare this film.

In 1996, after fifteen years and many films depicting gay and lesbian themes, writer-director Richard Kwietniowski, made *Love and Death on Long Island.* This story involves an aging British writer, Giles De'Ath. Giles becomes smitten with a young American actor, Ronnie Bostock, when he accidentally sees Bostock in a film *Hot Pants College II* at a multiplex cinema where he had hoped to see *A Passage to India* , which is based on the novel by the gay author, E. M. Forster. At this time in his career, De'Ath's reputation as an author is somewhat shaky. His agent encourages him to take a vacation. After researching Bostock's life and career, primarily from teen-oriented magazines, De'Ath travels to Long Island to find Bostock. There he engineers a meeting with Bostock's girlfriend, Audrey, by ramming into her shopping cart in a supermarket. Through Audrey, De'Ath meets Bostock, befriends him, and heaps praises on Bostock's lackluster talent. Towards the end of the film De'Ath proposes to devote his life to Bostock's career and confesses his love for him. Bostock departs abruptly and rejects De'Ath's offer and affections. After Bostock receives a very long letter via fax from the aging writer, he does, however, incorporate Shakespeare into his films as De'Ath had wished.

Reviewer Patricia Kowal praised *Love and Death on Long Island* as a "rich blend of Thomas Mann's *Death in Venice* and Nabokov's *Lolita.*" She wrote:

> While both Humbert Humbert and Giles De'Ath find themselves driven down the ladder of social strata by lust, one is tragically destroyed by it, the other miraculously resurrected . . . Giles is sparked back to life through this "insane" crush . . . [an] infatuation with someone that he might otherwise revile. Ultimately the film is a bittersweet exploration of the power of love, even unrequited love, as well as the power of the cinema to shape our fantasies and or expectations.

Nonetheless the film tends to reinforce beliefs that relationships between older men and a younger men are neither desirable sexually nor appropriate socially. At least Giles doesn't die at the end of the film, like Aschenbach or the principal lesbian or gay characters of such films from the 1960s or 1970s as *The Fox, The Children's Hour,* and *Dog Day Afternoon.* De'Ath is portrayed in the film as a silly anachronism of his time. He doesn't own a computer or a VCR at the beginning of the film. He pursues his obsession with Bostock through awkward gestures. When he finally reveals his love to Bostock, he is flatly rejected. Ronnie returns to his girlfriend. Giles goes to the beach and stares at the sea, pondering his life and misfortune. But he doesn't die.

Gods and Monsters, released in 1998, is a film loosely based on a novel by Christopher Brahm, about James Whale, the creator of the original Frankenstein movies. In this film, Whale is portrayed as a fading film director, whose career was ruined by a homosexual scandal. His mind is deteriorating after a series of strokes. Nevertheless he still has a penchant for young men. He insists that a young film student who comes to interview him, remove an article of clothing, as Whale's compensation for answering each question. Whale, subsequently, becomes smitten with his new groundskeeper, Clayton Boone, a reject from the Marines during the Korean War. Whale invites Clayton to pose for him while he sketches. At first Whale denies being homosexual, but then reveals the truth about his sexual orientation in erotic details to Clayton, who becomes annoyed with Whales suggestive "locker room" talk. Clayton doesn't reject Whale completely as Ronnie did Giles in *Love and Death on Long Island.* Towards the end of the film they tussle when Whale in a ghoulish fashion attempts to seduce Boone whom he asks to wear a gas mask from World War I while posing in the nude. After Boone frees himself from the mask he almost strangles Whale. But he pulls back, breaks down and cries. Boone later tucks Whale into bed. That night Whale takes his own life and is found dead floating in his swimming pool not unlike the young writer, Joe Gillis, who is shot by the aging actress Norma Desmond at the beginning of the movie *Sunset Boulevard.* If there is any equality in Hollywood's handling of inter-generational relationships as represented by these two films, it is that neither homosexual nor heterosexual intergenerational relationships can be consummated sexually and must ultimately be punished in death.

Theater and film critic Jan Stuart wrote the following in a review of *Gods and Monsters* in the October 27, 1998 issue of *The Advocate:*

> Unrequited gay-straight May-September Yank-Brit love stories would appear to be this year's flavor, but Condon's fictionalized bio [in his film *Gods and Monsters*] is head and shoulders above *Love and Death on Long Island* as a subtle psychological study of the mutual dependency of two unlikely soul mates. Poetic spirits from rough-and-tumble backgrounds, Whale and Boone share an

instinctive empathy for the other's solitude, which is expressed with increasing tenderness and ferocity as the director's condition deteriorates.

Lest we assume that Boone's sexuality might have in some way been influenced by the tenderness of his relationship with Whale, the audience is assured at the end of the film that Boone has safely been tucked into a life of heterosexual marriage and family. At the end of the film we see Boone, after watching one of Whale's movies on television with his son, showing him an original sketch of a Frankenstein monster.

REVIEW OF THE LITERATURE ON INTERGENERATIONAL GAY MALE RELATIONSHIPS

In searching for research articles or historical models for intergenerational relationships between older gay men and younger men, I discovered that such relationships are almost entirely framed in terms of adult-child relationships (pedophilia) or adult-adolescent-relationships (ephebophilia). The 1991 anthology, *Male Intergenerational Intimacy* (Sandfort, Brongersma & van Naerseen) is devoted entirely to man-boy relationships, from historical, socio-psychological, and legal perspectives. In this volume, Gerald P. Jones, wrote that the research on intergenerational intimacy, social as well as sexual was frequently labeled "child sexual abuse," which he claimed fostered a "one-sided, simplistic picture of intergenerational intimacy." Jones pointed out that a close look at such studies revealed two flaws: the studies nearly always maintained a narrow focus on sexual contact, and proceeded from the assumption that sexual contact in intergenerational relationships by definition constituted abuse. Jones commented that little distinction was made in such research about relationships between adults and children and relationships between adults and adolescents, even those of a consenting age, roughly between sixteen and eighteen years of age in the United States. Research which refuted the prevailing belief that adult-minor relationships (sometimes even suggesting that such consensual relationships might even be beneficial to the young persons involved) was often ignored or suppressed.

I contend that framing all intergenerational relationships as abuse or as an imbalance of power colors perceptions about and limits interest in researching such relationships even when the partners are consenting adults of different ages.

In searching through all of the volumes of the *Journal of Homosexuality,* from 1977 to the present, I found only one pertinent research article: "Decision-Making and Age Differences Among Gay Male Couples," by Joseph Harry. When Harry (1983) asked the 1,556 respondents to his questionnaire what the preferred age of their partners was, most said they preferred men of their own age, except for the youngest group (under 25) and the oldest group (over 39), although even their preferences rarely reached beyond 10 years of their own age. Harry's research also indicated that when older men are partnered with younger men, older men made decisions more often than their younger partners. However, Harry was quick to point out that "difference in age is not sufficient to ensure an inegalitarian relationship." For example, few of Harry's respondents were involved in relationships where one was financially dependent on the other.

David McWhirter and Andrew Mattison (1984), themselves an intergenerational couple with a sixteen-year age difference, found in their study of 156 gay male couples in the San Diego area, that the couples with the greatest relationship longevity were those that also had the greatest differences in ages. All of the couples who were together for longer than 30 years (8 couples) had age differences from between five to sixteen years.

In couples with more than 10 years age difference who have been together for more than five years, the age difference is usually of more concern to the older partner than to the younger man. These couples talk of the complementarity they find in each other. They learn from each other, with the older partner providing direction and stability for the younger. These couples do express more elements of sexual disharmony than others do, however.

Richard Isay (1996), author of *Becoming Gay,* found elderly gay men were less inclined than heterosexuals to view age-discrepant relationships as inappropriate. Four of the eight gay elderly gay clients he worked with reported having benefited from being in relationships of five or more years with partners who were twenty to thirty years younger. Isay concluded:

> While it may be the affluence of the older partner that initially attracts a younger man, and the youthful qualities that initially attract the older man to the younger, it appears to be the "intrinsic qualities" of each, such as loyalty, honesty, and trustworthiness, that make these relationships endure. (p. 151)

Steinman in his study (1983-85) of 46 gay male relationships whose age discrepancies ranged from 8 to 40 years (with a median age gap of 14 years), found that couples with age discrepancies of 11 years or less were more than twice as likely to have relationships which had endured at least four years, when compared to couple with greater age gaps. They attempted in their study to prove the hypothesis that older men offered their younger partners extrinsic resources such as material possessions and money, while younger men offered intrinsic resources such as their physical attractiveness and sexual appeal.

What Steinman discovered, however, was that though this pattern was true for some couples, it was not consistent overall. A number of couples made a concerted effort to equalize their differences in material wealth by the young partner making more in-kind contributions to household necessities, such as labor or paying for household expenses versus paying the mortgage. Younger partners had difficulties keeping up with the spending habits of their older partners. Younger partners exercised some control over their sexual relationship by refusing sex to their older partners who generally showed a greater interest in sex.

HISTORICAL EXAMPLES
OF INTERGENERATIONAL RELATIONSHIPS

Anthropologists Gilbert Herdt (1984) and Walter Williams (1986) suggested that intergenerational relationships have long histories in indigenous cultures in Melanesia as well as North America. Other examples can be found in historical and cultural studies of Greece (Dover, 1989), Japan (Watanabe & Iwata, 1989) and China (Hinsch, 1990). In nineteenth- and twentieth-century European and American history, some notable examples of intergenerational relationships can be found. According to Leigh Rutledge's *The Gay Book of Lists* (Routledge, 1987), poet Walt Whitman, for instance, was 46 when he met streetcar driver, Peter Doyle, who was then 18. Their relationship lasted for eight years although their correspondence continued until close to the end of Whitman's life in 1892. Charlie Shively (1987) wrote of the differences in their ages:

> Pete had been a teenager when he met Walt, who was nearing fifty. As Peter grew older, he was no longer a boy; and as Walt grew older, he began to suffer the infirmities of age. The strains of his relationship with Peter interwove with his own deteriorating health

and his mother's death. Whitman suffered a stroke on January 23, 1873, in Washington. In 1889, the poet recalled Doyle and told Horace Traubel, "I wonder where he is now. He must have got another lay [sic]. How faithful he was in those sick times–coming every day in his spare hours to my room–doing chores–going for medicine, making bed, somewhat like that and never growling." Convalescing from his stroke and the shock of his mother's death in May, 1873, Whitman retired to his brother's house in Camden, New Jersey. He never rejoined Peter.

Writer W. Somerset Maugham was forty when he met his partner of twenty-nine years, Gerald Haxton who was age 22, on the Flanders front during World War I. Haxton became Maugham's secretary, companion, and lover, the outgoing intermediary for the shy writer during their international travels. Their relationship, however, proved to be difficult, as Haxton was alcoholic, violent, dishonest, and unfaithful. Haxton died in 1944 from an ulcer. When he was 72 Maugham subsequently took another younger lover, Alan Searle, who was then 41. Searle also served as Maugham's secretary and proved to be more loyal, and mild mannered than his predecessor, Haxton. Their relationship lasted 19 years. Maugham adopted Searle as his son in an attempt to cut his daughter, Elizabeth, out of his will. But his daughter had the adoption nullified and had herself restored as the writer's legal heir.

Psychiatrist Harry Stack Sullivan was 35 years old when he met a young man named James Inscot, who was 15 or 16 at the time (Allen, 1995). Inscot later adopted Sullivan's last name as his own and became known as his "foster son," living with the psychologist for 22 years, serving as Sullivan's secretary, housekeeper, office manager, and longtime companion until Harry's death in 1949. Inscot inherited the psychologist's entire estate.

Author Christopher Isherwood was 48 years old when he met painter and illustrator Don Bachardy who was then 18 in 1951. Their relationship lasted thirty-two years. Of their relationship biographer Jonathan Fryer (1977) wrote:

> Christopher watched lovingly over the artistic and character development of the younger man, helping where he could, but not crushing Don's sensibility with his own forceful personality and his standing as a writer. He encouraged Don in his own branch of creativity, as well as working directly with him in the latter years. Don, in turn, provided moral support and a sense of stability, while

accepting Christopher's outlook on other [sexual] relationships. They share the mundane necessities of everyday jobs, such as housework, and by preference chose new friendships that both could enjoy. (p. 286)

Contact between men of different generations was more common prior to World War II. There were fewer public spaces available for gays to congregate. Consequently, gay men introduced each other through their friends. In *The Other Side of Silence,* John Laughery (1998) discussed the tradition of "aunties" in pre-World War II gay communities:

What a gay man in his teens or twenties couldn't often get from his peers was a feeling for the ways in which his sexuality might take on the dimensions of a full life outside the mainstream. In this realm, the "aunties" were indispensable. The terms itself implies a brutal age consciousness (one could pass from the "belle" to the "auntie" stage by thirty or thirty-five), but the reality is that most gay men approaching or well into, middle age during the pre-World War II period did not consider themselves out of the running. The first blush of youth might have passed, but not the urge to party, advise, camp, cruise, take a lover, find a mate. And the knowledge and encouragement they had to offer younger homosexual men were valued by many of their charges. (p 112)

Parties during this period, Laughery contends, were more intergenerational than they were in the 1980s or 1990s.

Intergenerational friendships provided for homosexuals in the 1930s a sense that they were part of a continuum, a social order with a meaningful life that would outline its participants. This vital cultural transmission often included a bit of instruction about responsibilities in the decades to come. In other words, how nice to be young, but of course time moves on, and the help you receive today is to be extended to others in later years. The comely twenty-year-old taken out to dinner by his friend of forty-five or sixty, introduced to other gay men (thus easing his fear of isolation, or freakishness) brought to the theater, or taught how to camp or deal with the police or employers or how not to drop hairpins, was made aware that he, in turn, should "give something back" when the time came. The older man paid the bill at the restaurant, made the introductions, provided the useful tips in what might have been a sexual or a platonic relationship, or something in between in a manner fundamentally different, in this instance from the male-female pattern. Part of the younger man's repayment to the aunties was tied to the notion that he would someday assume the same role for others. . . . (p. 117)

Social patterns in gay male communities today are more age segregated. Bars are frequented by men of a particular age range. Gay youth centers have been designed of those persons under 21 who are beginning to explore their sexual orientation or gender identity. Some intergenerational opportunities exist through publications, such as *Chiron Rising, Daddy,* and the publications for Bears (hairy men and their admirers). Prime Timers, a social network of chapters established internationally for "mature gay and bisexual men and their admirers," provides opportunities for older men and younger men to meet, socialize, and date. A proliferation of web sites on the Internet (see Resources) also offer greater access world wide for older and younger men to meet and for middle-aged and older men to meet.

The lack of films or books (outside the arena of erotic materials), however, limits the possibilities for younger men to envision what it is like to be old. Few films, stories, or research articles or even to suggest that sometimes it is the younger men who pursue older men rather than the reverse. Imagine a film portraying a twenty-five year old who pursues a sixty-year old man. After an initial fling, the older man tells the younger man to find a partner closer to his own age, as the older man prefers being with his peers. Or imagine a filmmaker chronicling the history of one of the notable men mentioned previously (Christopher Isherwood and Don Bachardy, for instance) to show a viewing audience how a relationship between men of different generations matures over time.

In order to understand the value of intergenerational relationships and the challenges that the partners in those relationships face, I placed notices on the Bears mailing list and the Twin Cities chapter of Prime Timers newsletter, inviting couples to tell their stories. I received a dozen responses from couples willing to do so. It should be noted that these accounts are stories of successful relationships. I did not receive, nor did I seek out, examples of intergenerational relationships which failed. Below, I present brief accounts of five couples; each couple had an age difference of at least twelve years.

Phil (age 55) and Raymond (age 33). Phil and Raymond met ten years ago when both had other partners. Three years ago they re-met, as single men. Phil had divorced. Ray's lover had died from AIDS. On their first date they disclosed to each other that they both were HIV-positive. In May of 1999 they held a commitment-marriage ceremony at the Episcopal Cathedral they attend in Portland, Oregon. Of their relationship Phil wrote:

> The age difference between us has worked to our advantage. Raymond is need of stability and emotional security; and I give that to him. He is passive and I am sexually aggressive and very sexual. We both have friends our own age that we do things with: I belong to a motorcycle club and Raymond loves to ride with me. He likes contemporary music and I like classical. He goes to concerts with friends or my daughter. I like to go to art house movies. This relationship is much easier because I had almost thirty years of marriage in which to mature, to learn to cut down the need to control and to discover from trial and error what works.

> We often say that this is the best time of our lives because we have each other. We play cards and exchange dinners with another couple where one is forty-eight and the other thirty-two; and like us, the older man was married and has two sons.

> The age difference really works to our advantage. I thank God for sending me Raymond. He makes me feel like a kid again. And he is a great grandma to our grand kids!

Arimo (51 years) and Nino (27 years). Arimo and Nino met at a New Year's party in 1995 in Helsinki, Finland. They live about 500 kilometers apart in the towns of Kuopio in eastern Finland and Turku in southern Finland. Nino said of Arimo:

> I have always been attracted to older men, large, furry, bearded Bears like Arimo. And he has always liked men younger and slimmer than himself. We are like day and night in almost every physical and mental sense. Yet on some level we share a common ground, being a combination of "otherness" and "familiarity."

Arimo said:

> Having a relationship with a much younger partner helps me maintain a vital attitude. Through Nino's influence I have also been ex-

posed to the world of the younger generation and learned things I probably would not have learned otherwise. I have also been able to impart some of my experience to Nino. Our relationship has a strong teacher-student aspect all of the time. For instance, I encourage Nino to study French which he probably would not have done without me. We also enjoy the "dad-son" aspects of our relationship although most of the time we are completely equal partners.

They also recognize the negative aspects of their age differences. Arimo will probably die much before Nino. Nevertheless they maintain that the positive aspects of their age differences far outweigh the negative ones.

Steve (age 58) and Jim (age 46). Steve and Jim met in August of 1994. By November of that year, they were in a monogamous committed relationship. They hosted their wedding on August 15, 1995, and moved in together (with Jim's twin sons, age 15). The last twin moved out in February of 1997, so there is now, as Jim describes it "deep quiet to their house." Jim wrote of their relationship:

After living most of my life in the guise of a heterosexual marriage, I find being with Steven has been the very best time of my life as well as the most fulfilling. We are both good cooks which makes it necessary for us to watch our weight. We both enjoy theater and have season tickets for three play houses.

Regarding our age difference: We are friends with several couples who have notable age differences. One gay couple is thirty-five years apart. Another is fifteen years apart. A straight couple is sixteen years apart. A lesbian couple is 8 years apart. So our experience indicates that these age differences are not uncommon in any population we are familiar with.

Steve believes that he will outlive me. I sometimes wonder if I will be left alone. I hope we have many years of good health together.

Stephen (age 49) and Scott (age 36). Stephen and Scott met nine years ago on a hike in the Cascade mountains of Washington. They were married in a ceremony at Spirit of the Lakes United Church of Christ in Minneapolis in September 18, 1993. Scott says:

I always was better able to get along with older folks than my peers. I had been in other relationships with older men, but felt more like the object in those relationships. In our relationship Stephen doesn't seem as old as he is; and I don't act as young as I am. We have moved in our relationship from being more complementary to being more similar to each other. Being with Stephen has encouraged me to prepare for my twilight years by doing some financial planning.

Stephen says:

I am seven years younger than Scott's parents. I try to maintain a respectful boundary around my age with Scott parents. We tend to have friends who are more my age, especially straight couple friends. I am attracted to Scott's playfulness, outrageousness, and his enjoyment of physical affection. We devote at least a half-hour each day to comedy routines and tickling. We have the happiest relationship of any of our [straight] siblings. In a few years I might consider a monastic vocation, which would change the nature of our relationship. For me it would be a tradeoff to serve the community versus being visible as a gay couple.

Wally (age 71) and Randall (age 37). Wally began the Twin Cities chapter of Prime Timers, a social club and international network for "mature gay and bisexual men and their younger male admirers." Within a couple of months, the club membership grew to over 100 and now has 120 members. Wally is a retired band director of high schools in England and other countries. He is a widower with four adult daughters and five grandchildren. Randall was trained as a gourmet chef, hosts a Prime Timers cooking group, and now makes his living in the computer industry. Wally says of his relationship with Randall:

Six years ago I met Randall, a person that has come to mean a very great deal to me, so much so that we decided two years ago to buy a house together. There is a great gap in our ages but we are soul mates at heart and have great times together. We share many common interests (concerts, shows, plays, spectator sports) and must guard against being too insular or self-contained. I cherish our relationship and look forward to the things we have planned. When I finally grow up, I would like to be a philanthropist. If that doesn't work out, maybe I'll try alchemy.

CONCLUSIONS

From this study I conclude that few cultural representations of relationships between older gay men and younger men exist. There has been little change over thirty years in how such relationships are portrayed in film. Films such as *Death in Venice, Love and Death on Long Island,* and *Gods and Monsters* depict the vulnerability of the old who are attracted to the young. Relationships between the two are sometimes seen as tender but ultimately result in frustrated and unrequited love and sometimes the death of the older man. Little research has been done to study the impact of age differences between adult gay men. Most research on intergenerational relationships have focused on relationships between adult men and children or adolescents. The few studies that have been published on relationships between adult gay men of differing ages have demonstrated that intergenerational relationships have been beneficial for the participants of these studies, and that the value of such relationships have more to do with intrinsic qualities shared between partners than their extrinsic age or differences in material wealth and experience.

More research is needed both of historical examples of intergenerational relationships as well as from contemporary couples to understand the value and challenges for the persons involved in these relationships. If literature and film presented a more balanced, complex, and positive view of such relationships, this would help to overcome the negative stereotypes portrayed in existing films. The combination of research and artistic expression can challenge the explicit ageism and homophobia that casts a negative view of intergenerational gay male relationships . Such scholarly and artistic endeavors could help gay men see the value of relationships with older or younger men and to diminish the stigma for those already involved in intergenerational relationships.

REFERENCES

Allen, M. (1995). Sullivan's closet: A reappraisal of Harry Stack Sullivan's life and his pioneering role in American psychiatry. *Journal of Homosexuality*, 29(1), 1-17.

Byron, St. (1971, July 18). Finally two films dealing with the issues of gay lib. *Village Voice 11*:11:1 In *The New York Times Film Reviews 1971-1972.* (1973) New York: The New York Times and Arno Press. 102-103.

Calder, R. (1989). *Willie: The life of W. Somerset Maugham.* London: Heineman.

Dover, J. R. (1989). *Greek homosexuality.* Cambridge, MA: Harvard University Press.

Fryer, J. (1977). *Isherwood: A biography of Christopher Isherwood*. London: New English Library.

Georges, G. E. (1998). [Review of the film *Gods and Monsters*] In Banks, M. (Ed.) *Magill's Cinema Annual 1999*. Detroit, MI: The Gale Group. 177-179.

Harry, J. (1982). Decision-making and age differences among gay male couples. *Journal of Homosexuality 8*(2):9-21.

Herdt, G. (1984). *Ritualized homosexuality in Melanesia*. Berkeley, CA: University of California Press.

Hinsch, G. (1990). *Passions of the cut sleeve: The male homosexual tradition in China*. Berkeley, CA: University of California Press.

Isay, R. (1996). *Becoming gay*. New York: Henry Holt and Company.

Jones, G. (1991). The study of intergenerational intimacy in North America: Beyond politics and pedophilia. In T. Sandfort, E. Brongersma, & A. van Naerssen (Eds.), *Male intergenerational intimacy: Historical, socio-psychological, and legal perspectives* (pp. 275-296). New York: Harrington Park Press.

Kowal, P. (1998). [Review of the film *Love and Death on Long Island*.] In Banks, M. (Ed.) *Magill's Cinema Annual 1999*. Detroit, MI: The Gale Group. 310-311.

Laughery, J. (1998). *The other side of silence*. New York: Henry Holt and Co.

Mann, T. (1998) *Death in Venice and other tales*. New York: Penguin Putnam, Inc.

McWhirter, D., & Mattison, A. (1984). *The male couple*. Englewood Cliffs, NJ: Prentice-Hall, Inc.

Perry, H. (1982). *Psychiatrist of America: The life of Harry Stack Sullivan*. Cambridge, MA: Belknap Press.

Routledge, L. (1987). *The gay book of lists*. Boston: Alyson Publications.

Shively, C. (1987). *Calamus lovers: Walt Whitman's working class camerados*. San Francisco: Gay Sunshine Press.

Steinman, R. (1991). Social exchanges between older and younger gay male partners. In Lee, J. (Ed.), *Gay midlife and maturity* (pp. 179-206). New York: Harrington Park Press.

Stuart, J. (1998, October 27) Yes, sir. *Advocate 771*:75.

Watanabe, T., & Iwata, J. *Love of the Samurai: A thousand years of Japanese homosexuality*. London: GMP.

Williams, W. (1986) *Spirit and the flesh*. Boston: Beacon Press.

ON-LINE RESOURCES:

The Grey Gay Guide:
    http://www.ourworld.compuserv.com/homepage/Pewit/greygay1.htm
Mature Men:
    http://www.maturemen.org/lists
Older Younger Connections Links:
    http://www.geocities/com/WestHollywood/Stonewall/2028/links.htm
Pink and Grey:
    http://www.pinkngrey.com

Retirement Intentions of Same-Sex Couples

Steven E. Mock

SUMMARY. Retirement intentions of same-sex and opposite-sex couples were investigated. Data were drawn from the Cornell Couples and Careers Study. The sample consists of 32 women in same-sex relationships, 7 men in same-sex relationships, 30 men and women in cohabiting relationships, and 30 married men and women. Participants' responses to such questions as age expected to retire, age they began retirement planning, degree of financial planning for retirement, degree of preparation for housing and healthcare, and plans for post-retirement work and volunteering were analyzed. Female same-sex couples self-rate on financial planning for retirement to a significantly lower degree than married couples. The implications for post-retirement well-being and the need for financial planning are discussed. *[Article copies available for a fee from The Haworth Document Delivery Service: 1-800-HAWORTH. E-mail address: <getinfo@haworthpressinc.com> Website: <http://www.HaworthPress.com> © 2001 by The Haworth Press, Inc. All rights reserved.]*

KEYWORDS. Same-sex couples, opposite-sex couples, retirement, retirement planning, retirement intentions, financial planning

Retirement is a significant turning point in adulthood (Moen, 1996), and this transition requires some degree of planning. Often the planning

Steven E. Mock is affiliated with Cornell University.

Address correspondence to: Steven E. Mock, Department of Human Development, MVR Hall, Cornell University, Ithaca, NY 14853-4401 (E-mail: sem33@cornell.edu).

[Haworth co-indexing entry note]: "Retirement Intentions of Same-Sex Couples." Mock, Steven E. Co-published simultaneously in *Journal of Gay & Lesbian Social Services* (Harrington Park Press, an imprint of The Haworth Press, Inc.) Vol. 13, No. 4, 2001, pp. 81-86; and: *Midlife and Aging in Gay America* (ed: Douglas C. Kimmel, and Dawn Lundy Martin) Harrington Park Press, an imprint of The Haworth Press, Inc., 2001, pp. 81-86. Single or multiple copies of this article are available for a fee from The Haworth Document Delivery Service [1-800-HAWORTH, 9:00 a.m. - 5:00 p.m. (EST). E-mail address: getinfo@haworthpressinc.com].

is done not only in the context of individual needs, but with the needs of one's partner and family in mind. Based on today's realities, it is necessary to take a flexible view of the definition of "families" and "couple" (Esterberg & Savin-Williams, 2000). This flexible view includes a consideration of gay and lesbian people as they and their partners plan for the future (Peplau, 1994). This exploratory study examines the retirement planning of same-sex couples in comparison with cohabiting and married opposite-sex couples.

METHOD

Participants

Data for this study were drawn from the Couples and Careers Study (Moen, 1998), a study of dual-career couples conducted at the Cornell Employment and Family Careers Institute. Participants were contacted through their workplace and in hour-long telephone interviews, both partners were asked (in separate interviews) to report their family, work, and biographical experiences.

Thirty-two women and seven men comprise the same-sex couples in the Cornell Couples and Careers Study; all are in relationships. The average age of the women is 38 ($SD = 6$, range = 26 to 57), and 48 for the men ($SD = 6$, range = 42 to 59). The average individual income for women is $48,000 ($SD = \$20,000$, min = $11,000, max = $95,000) and for the men is $50,000 ($SD = \$22,512$, min = $12,000, max = $67,000). Twenty-eight of the women are European American/white (non-Hispanic), one is African-American, one is Hispanic, and one is multi-ethnic. All the men are European American/white (non-Hispanic). (See Table 1.)

For the basis of comparison in an Analysis of Variance (ANOVA), 15 cohabiting opposite-sex couples and fifteen married couples were matched with the same-sex couples on demographic variables including income, education, age, and number of children. Previous couples research indicates that there are qualitative differences in the experiences of male and female same-sex couples as well as cohabiting and married opposite-sex couples (Blumstein & Schwarz, 1983).

Materials. Questions selected for analysis were age expected to retire, the age they began retirement planning, and several retirement planning questions. Retirement planning is assessed with the following questions: "On a scale of 0 to 100 where 0 is none and 100 is a lot, how much planning have you done in each of the following areas to prepare

TABLE 1. Comparison of Same-Sex and Opposite-Sex Couples (N = 99)

Individuals	n	Mean Age	Mean Income ($)
Same-Sex			
Women	32	38	48,000
Men	7	48	50,500
Opposite-Sex			
Cohabiting	30	42	50,000
Married	30	41	50,500

Source: Moen (1998).

for retirement: financial preparation, learning about retirement or health insurance options, considering housing arrangements, planning for health care needs, thought about 2nd or 3rd career, and thinking about volunteer work?"

The relationships between retirement planning and income, type of employment, and type of couple were analyzed, first with ANOVA, then with linear contrasts and post-hoc comparisons when appropriate to determine which groups differed.

RESULTS

An analysis of variance showed that age expected to retire and age one began retirement planning were not significantly different between the groups. Similarly, for degree of consideration of retirement/insurance options, degree of consideration of housing options, and planning for health care needs, there was no effect for type of couple. These analyses were also run without the male same-sex couples (due to the limited n and high variance of this group) with similar results. (See Table 2.)

However, in a linear contrast, when compared with the three other couple types, married couples have a higher rating of planning for post-retirement volunteering, though not to a significant degree, $t(95) = -1.95$, $p = .055$. When analyzed including the male same-sex couples,

TABLE 2. Retirement Plans (N = 99)

Individuals Age Expect to Retire		Age Began Planning	Degree of Post-Ret. Volunteering (%)	Degree of Financial Preparation (%)
Same-Sex				
Women	59	30	48	54
Men	60	35	47	60
Opposite-Sex				
Cohabiting	59	34	46	62
Married	60	32	63*	75**

* trend, greater than other three groups to a degree approaching significance p = .055
** significantly greater than female same-sex couples, p < .05
Source: Moen (1998).

type of couple did not have a significant effect on rating of financial preparation, F (3,95) = 1.503, p = .055. When the rating of financial preparation was analyzed without the male same-sex couples, type of couple had a significant effect, F (2,89) = 3.95, p < .05. For both analyses including and excluding the male same-sex couples, post hoc comparisons revealed a significant difference between the female same-sex couples and the married couples (Tukey HSD, p < .05).[1] (See Figure 1.)

DISCUSSION

Similarity and difference. The same-sex and opposite-sex couples in this study share many characteristics in their patterns of retirement planning. For example, they plan to retire at similar ages, began the planning process at similar times in their lives, and are planning for healthcare and housing needs to a similar degree. However, married couples have a higher self-rating of post-retirement volunteering than the other couples, to a degree approaching significance. Furthermore, female same-sex couples have a mean self-rating of degree of financial preparation lower than the other three groups, and significantly lower than the married couples.

FIGURE 1. Self-Rating of Degree of Financial Planning for Retirement

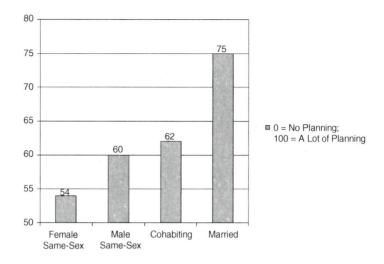

Source: Cornell Couples and Careers Study (1998), *N* = 99

Implications for post-retirement well-being. Post-retirement work and volunteering are associated with greater well-being (Kim & Moen, 1999). Thus, these results imply that male and female same-sex couples and heterosexual cohabiting couples may be at a disadvantage in this regard when compared with married couples. Perhaps more important is the low rating of degree of financial preparation by the female same-sex couples. It is possible that many of the female same-sex couples believe they have an adequate workplace pension, or they might be self-rating more conservatively for some other reason. Previous literature suggests that women plan less for retirement than men, though in this study, there was no effect found for gender on rating of financial preparation, indicating that the difference found is due more to the nature of couple type than gender alone. The lower self-rating of degree of financial preparation for retirement may point to a need for greater financial planning.

Though the participants in this study are affluent and are not representative of the experiences of all couples, the low rating of financial preparation by female same-sex couples in an affluent sample emphasizes the need to examine this issue with a less affluent sample. Current research at the Careers Institute investigates why the female same-sex couples are rating their degree of financial planning lower to determine whether this finding is a result of a self-report bias or indicates a need for increased financial planning.

ACKNOWLEDGMENTS

The data for this research were drawn from the Couples and Careers Study: Cornell Employment and Family Careers Institute, funded by the Alfred P. Sloan Foundation (Grant Numbers: Sloan FDN 96-6-9 and 99-6-3), Phyllis Moen, Principal Investigator. The results of this study were originally presented at the SAGE Conference, Fordham University, NY, May 2000. The author gratefully acknowledges the assistance of Phyllis E. Moen, Stephen Sweet, Ritch C. Savin-Williams, and Noelle A. Chesley.

NOTE

1. A regression analysis was run predicting degree of financial preparation from couple type, controlling for salary, age, and subject number. Subject numbers are shared by each couple in the data set and were added to the model to control for the fact that this is paired data. It was found that type of couple was significant, F, (3.84), $p < .05$, and in pairwise comparisons female same-sex couples rated financial planning significantly lower than married couples, $p < .01$.

REFERENCES

Blumstein, P., & Schwarz, P. (1983). *American couples.* New York: William Morrow.
Kim, J. E., & Moen, P. (1999). *Work/retirement transitions and psychological well-being in late midlife.* Unpublished manuscript.
Moen, P. (1996). A life course perspective on retirement, gender, and well-being. *Journal of Occupational Health Psychology, 1,* 131-144.
Moen, P. (1998). *Cornell couples and careers study.* Ithaca, NY: Cornell University, Cornell Employment and Family Careers Institute.
Peplau, L. (1994). Men and women in love. In D. L. Sollie & L. A. Leslie (Eds.), *Gender, families, and close relationships: Feminist research journeys* (pp. 19-49). Thousand Oaks, CA: Sage Publications.
Savin-Williams, R. C., & Esterberg, K. G. (2000). Lesbian, Gay, and Bisexual families, in D. H. Demo, K. R. Allen, & M. A. Fine (Eds.), *Handbook of Family Diversity* (pp. 197-215). New York: Oxford University Press.

Preliminary Study of Caregiving and Post-Caregiving Experiences of Older Gay Men and Lesbians

Kristina Hash

SUMMARY. This qualitative study expands the existing family caregiving model to include the unique experiences of older gay men and lesbians caring for chronically ill, same-sex partners. In-depth interviews of four caregivers focused on the strains and positive aspects involved in caregiving and following the cessation of care. The analysis of preliminary interviews revealed that respondents had similar experiences as those in previous caregiving studies (including physical, financial and emotional strains). The unique aspects of their experiences, however, involved interactions with formal and informal support persons, attitudes towards helping professionals, disclosure of the relationship, and long-term planning and decision-making. *[Article copies available for a fee from The Haworth Document Delivery Service: 1-800-HAWORTH. E-mail address: <getinfo@haworthpressinc.com> Website: <http://www.HaworthPress.com> © 2001 by The Haworth Press, Inc. All rights reserved.]*

KEYWORDS. Caregiving, gay men, lesbians, older, chronic illness, same sex partners, support, professionals, long-term planning, post-caregiving

---

Kristina Hash, MSW, is a PhD Candidate, Virginia Commonwealth University. Address correspondence to: Kristina Hash, VCU School of Social Work, P.O. Box 842027, 1001 W. Franklin Street, Richmond, VA 23284-2027.

[Haworth co-indexing entry note]: "Preliminary Study of Caregiving and Post-Caregiving Experiences of Older Gay Men and Lesbians." Hash, Kristina. Co-published simultaneously in *Journal of Gay & Lesbian Social Services* (Harrington Park Press, an imprint of The Haworth Press, Inc.) Vol. 13, No. 4, 2001, pp. 87-94; and: *Midlife and Aging in Gay America* (ed: Douglas C. Kimmel, and Dawn Lundy Martin) Harrington Park Press, an imprint of The Haworth Press, Inc., 2001, pp. 87-94. Single or multiple copies of this article are available for a fee from The Haworth Document Delivery Service [1-800-HAWORTH, 9:00 a.m. - 5:00 p.m. (EST). E-mail address: getinfo@haworthpressinc.com].

It is estimated that there are almost a million older gay men residing in the United States and perhaps over a million older lesbians (Berger, 1996; Kehoe, 1986). Only since the late 1970s has there existed professional literature that focuses on the experiences of this special population of older adults. Even in this attention, the literature has primarily examined the adjustment of older gay men and lesbians to old age (Berger, 1996; Kehoe, 1988; Kimmel, 1978). As a result, very little is known about providing care for older gay men and lesbians.

What is known from studies of the general population is that caregivers often endure negative effects related to the provision of care. In the broadest sense, these effects have been characterized as a set of "physical, psychological or emotional, social, and financial problems" (George & Gwyther, 1986, p. 253). This can include loss of sleep, depression, physical ailments, conflicts with work and other family roles, isolation, and pressure on the relationship. HIV/AIDS caregiving studies have also found similar stressors in caregiving (Folkman, Cherney, & Christopher-Richards Catania, & Gagnon, 1994; Turner et al., 1994).

Although not as widely researched, when care-receivers die or are relocated, caregivers have both negative and positive experiences. The negative effects often include depression, isolation, and guilt. The positive outcomes related to the loss of the care-receiver include improved health and greater social involvement for the care-provider (Shultz et al., 1997).

While advancing our understanding of the phenomenon, previous caregiving studies have primarily reflected the experiences of white, middle-class, heterosexual caregivers. Although studies of caregiving for persons with HIV/AIDS include the experiences of gay men and lesbians, they are limited to persons forty years of age and under and focus mostly on gay men. The current study was begun to expand the caregiving model to include the experiences of older gay men and lesbians in providing care for older, chronically ill partners as well as their experiences following the death or relocation of the partner for whom they had cared. The following served as the preliminary research questions for the study: What are the strains involved in providing care for an older, chronically ill partner? What are the positive aspects of providing this care? What are the strains involved following the loss of a partner? What are the positive aspects following the cessation of care? It was hoped that through this inquiry, the unique aspects of caregiving for this population would be illuminated. This article presents the preliminary findings for the study, based upon the experiences of four study participants.

METHOD

Sample

The study sought to attain respondents who were 50 years of age or older and who were either current caregivers or former caregivers (post-caregivers) for chronically ill, same-sex partners. To recruit respondents for the study, advertisements for the study were placed in gay and lesbian newspapers and the bulletins of gay social and spiritual organizations. Advertisements were also sent to other gay and lesbian organizations, bookstores, social groups, and support groups, hospice agencies and support groups for persons with HIV/AIDS, and personal contacts of the researcher. Approximately 700 advertisements were sent to 150 individuals and agencies in five states (Virginia, North Carolina, West Virginia, Maryland, and New York) and the District of Columbia.

The preliminary sample consisted of one woman and three men who resided in the Northeast and Southeast United States. All respondents were post-caregivers, had some form of higher education, and appeared to be middle class in terms of socioeconomic status. They ranged in age from 50-62, and all were Caucasian. Three of the respondents were widowed, while one respondent had ceased providing care because her partner relocated to a sibling's home.

Data Collection and Analysis

Data were collected through in-depth, semi-structured interviews. Three of the interviews were face-to-face and one was conducted over the phone. Field notes were taken during the interviews and were later expanded through use of audiotapes of the interviews. Data were then analyzed through the use of a constant comparative method. This method was used to identify themes and to develop, refine, and show relationships between concepts; it was achieved through the simultaneous processes of coding and analyzing data (Taylor & Bogden, 1998).

PRELIMINARY FINDINGS

The general caregiving literature states that one person usually manages the bulk of caregiving responsibilities. This was the case in this study. Being the only caregiver produced physical strains including exhaustion, lack of sleep, poor eating habits, and physical struggles related to hands-on care. Respondents noted that they experienced isolation and decreased finances. Caregiving responsibilities also resulted in tension in the relationship with their care-needy partner and conflicts with job responsibilities. Following the cessation of care, respondents experienced decreased finances, the destruction of future plans made with their partner, isolation, and feelings of loneliness, loss, and depression.

As in studies of the general population, respondents noted positive aspects of caregiving and caregiving cessation. Positive aspects of caregiving included an opportunity to show love and maintain a commitment to a significant other. As one respondent remarked, "regardless if I lose my house, lose everything, he's worth it." Following the cessation of care, respondents also enjoyed improved physical health and increased social interaction.

Although describing experiences similar to those in previous caregiving studies, the respondents were also faced with unique issues related to the provision of care for and, eventually, the loss, or relocation of, a same-sex partner. These issues included their interactions with informal (family and friends) and formal (professionals) support persons, attitudes towards professionals and services, disclosure of the relationship, and long-term planning and decision making.

Informal and Formal Supports

The respondents dealt with family members, friends, and professionals who did not provide them with the support they needed during caregiving and post-caregiving. Three of the respondents mentioned family members who were not supportive during this difficult time. This inadequate support was likely due to a lack of acceptance of the same-sex relationship. Two respondents, for example, encountered great difficulty with their partners' adult children (children from previous heterosexual marriages). As one respondent recounted, "At the funeral when it came time to cover him up . . . they asked his daughter to cover him up and she refused . . . they asked his son to cover him up and he refused."

Fortunately in other cases, family members and friends were very supportive during caregiving and post-caregiving. Supportive friends brought over meals and ran errands. One respondent even describes his partner's mother as becoming more supportive during this time, as they shared caregiving duties and continued to console each other in bereavement. This was quite unusual, given the fact that she had not previously been accepting of the relationship. Similarly, another respondent was surprised when her sister, who never really approved of her same sex-relationship, would call to see if she was "OK" and recognized the painful loss of her twenty-five year relationship.

All four respondents described one or more negative experiences with professionals. The head nurse at the nursing home where his partner resided for a few weeks "really didn't like faggots" and "made no bones about it." Other staff members asked his partner's mother, who was over 80 years old, if her son was the "husband or the wife" in his relationship with the respondent. To make matters worse, these professionals were often armed with unfriendly institutional policies. For example, only "family members" could park for free while visiting loved ones in one hospital. The respondent explains, "maybe it's a small issue, but it upset me . . . I had the will, the power of attorney . . . everything . . . but because I was not a blood relative, I couldn't park." This same respondent also encountered unfriendly policies in bereavement, as the cemetery refused to inter his partner in the mausoleum plot they had purchased together because "two unrelated men could not share the same plot." After a heated discussion and his threat to sue, the cemetery manager made an exception to the rule. This exception would cost the respondent an additional $1,100.

Conversely, respondents also noted encountering supportive professionals during caregiving and following the cessation of care. These were physicians, nurses, social workers, and other professionals whom they felt "comfortable" with, and who were understanding and respectful of the relationship. Additionally, supportive professionals "bent the rules" and treated same-sex partners as "immediate family" as far as policies and decision-making were concerned.

Attitudes About Professionals and Services

Given these experiences, it is not surprising that the respondents did not anticipate receiving support from the professionals they encountered. One respondent felt as though he was truly "fortunate" to have found supportive professionals. Another noted that it is the "exception" when you encounter, for example, a physician who would want to discuss care issues with a same-sex partner. Instead, she said, "he would be looking around for the mother, sister, etc." Additionally, another respondent was surprised when he received support and acceptance from members of a grief support group.

Just as respondents were not expecting support from health (and re-lated) professionals, they were equally apprehensive about seeking sup-portive services. They were especially leery about joining caregiver or bereavement support groups. One respondent shared that he did not want to go to a "straight" support group because "maybe they would be supportive and maybe not." Another respondent echoed this sentiment by explaining, "I just didn't fit in with what they were dealing with" and "I could hardly bare my soul to them." Similarly, another respondent was apprehensive about having home health care come into their home because of fear about what the visitor would think of their homosexual relationship.

Disclosure of the Relationship

As the caregiving experience often required interactions with health professionals, the respondents were faced with disclosure issues related to their same-sex relationships. Their disclosure to these persons ranged from direct verbalization to the "don't ask, don't tell" approach. In at-tempt to be recognized as a significant other by the physicians, one re-spondent said she "would go through the generalizations" such as "she lives with me" or "I'm her best friend." Sometimes, the physicians would catch on to these hints. Another respondent, on the other hand, did not attempt disclosure with hospice staff but said, "they knew, with-out coming right out and asking . . . they knew he was at my home and that we were not related." The two other respondents were both "out" to their partners' physicians and one was very forthcoming with the home health staff.

Long-Term Planning and Decision-Making

During caregiving, the respondents were concerned about setting up health care advanced directives for their partners. One caregiver took preventative action in planning, as he and his partner drew up a will spe-cifically so that "none of the children could challenge it." Similarly, an-other couple drew up a living will because, according to the respondent, "he wanted to make sure no one interfered with the decisions I had to make." Interestingly, property and financial affairs were often separate, even though a caregiving partner may have had medical power of attor-ney or other decision-making authority. Even though she sought medi-cal power of attorney for her partner, one respondent claimed that she never wanted joint property ownership because she is "just too independent" and "didn't want any legal hassles." Another couple also had separate finances and his partner's mother handled her son's bill paying when he became ill. Yet another respondent shared that even though they did not own their home jointly, he was the executor of the estate when his partner died.

CONCLUSION

In this preliminary study, certain patterns and themes emerged. It is clear that the respondents experienced similar strains and positive aspects in caregiving and post-caregiving as caregivers in the general population. What is important in this study, however, are the unique contributors to strain as well as unique positive aspects of caregiving and post-caregiving for this population. It seems that unsupportive friends, family, and professionals had the ability to adversely affect and add to the strain experienced by the respondents, both before and after the loss of their partners. These persons were not accepting of, but were insensitive to, the relationship and the needs of the couple and caregiver. On the other hand, it appears that supportive and understanding friends, family, and professionals often served as buffers against the experience of strain. These persons were respectful of the relationship and available for emotional and physical assistance. It also appears that this support was generally not anticipated, as the respondents seem to expect to be faced with insensitive and unsupportive individuals. Their experiences, both positive and negative, may have also influenced "other issues," including attitudes towards professionals, disclosure, of the relationship, and long-term planning and decision making.

Future interviews will explore issues that were not well illuminated in the preliminary study, including the questions: What are the long-term plans and decisions that are made? How do respondents deal with unsupportive informal and formal support persons? What are changes that could be made in health and human services that would better attend to the special needs of older, same-sex partners? Additionally, greater effort will be taken to recruit current caregivers, women, and persons of color.

The hope is that the preliminary and future interviews, combined, will provide an understanding of the unique caregiving and post-caregiving experiences of older gay men and lesbians. With the ever-increasing population of older adults, health and social service professionals may find greater numbers of caregivers and care-receivers in need of a variety of health care services as well as social and financial supports. In order to provide effective services to future caregivers, it will require the knowledge of, and sensitivity to, the needs of diverse groups of older adults. Relying solely upon the existing body of caregiving literature that promotes a generalized (and heterosexual) caregiving model, can only adversely affect the assistance received by the growing numbers of gay and lesbian older adults.

REFERENCES

Berger, R. M. (1996). *Gay and gray: The older homosexual man* (2nd ed.). New York: The Haworth Press, Inc.

Folkman, S., Chesney, M. A., & Christopher-Richards, A. (1994). Stress and coping in caregiving partners of men with AIDS. *Psychiatric Clinics of North America, 17* (1), 35-53.

George, L. K., & Gwyther, L. P. (1986). Caregiver well-being: A multidimensional examination of family caregivers of demented adults. *Gerontologist, 26* (3), 253-259.

Kehoe, M. (1986). Lesbian over 65: A triply invisible minority. *Journal of Homosexuality, 12* (3/4), 139-152.

Kehoe, M. (1988). Lesbians over 60 speak for themselves. *Journal of Homosexuality, 16*(3/4), 1-111.

Kimmel, D. C. (1978). Adult development and aging: A gay perspective. *Journal of Social Issues, 34* (3), 113-305.

Shultz, R., Newsom, J. T., Fleissner, K., Decamp, A. R., & Nieboer, A. P. (1997). Effects of bereavement after family caregiving. *Aging and Mental Health, 1* (3), 269-282.

Taylor, S. J., & Bogdan, R. C. (1998). Introduction to qualitative research: A guidebook and resource (3rd ed.). New York: John Wiley & Sons, Inc.

Turner, H. A., Catania, J. A., & Gagnon, J. (1994). The prevalence of informal caregiving to persons with AIDS in the United States: Caregiver characteristics and their implications. *Social Science and Medicine, 38* (11), 1543-1552.

Vision and Older Adults

Carol Sussman-Skalka

SUMMARY. Adults often accept vision loss as a natural part of aging and do not seek help. According to the Lighthouse National Survey on Vision Loss, 17% of Americans age 45 and older report a vision problem and more than one-third is unaware of available services. Although help is available, many older adults and health and social service providers do not know what vision rehabilitation services are, where to access them, and how they benefit people with vision impairments. The stigma often associated with vision loss may also prevent people from seeking help. For many gay and lesbian older adults, the stigma may be compounded by concerns related to disclosing their sexual identity. Aggressive outreach is necessary to promote awareness of services and resources for all individuals regardless of race, ethnicity, or sexual orientation. Vision rehabilitation includes a variety of services that help people cope with vision loss and develop skills to continue active and productive lives. They can make a difference by reducing unnecessary functional disability, thereby improving quality of life. *[Article copies available for a fee from The Haworth Document Delivery Service: 1-800-HAWORTH. E-mail address: <getinfo@haworthpressinc.com> Website: <http://www.HaworthPress.com> © 2001 by The Haworth Press, Inc. All rights reserved.]*

Carol Sussman-Skalka, CSW, MBA, is Director of Special Projects at Lighthouse International.

Address correspondence to: Carol Sussman-Skalka, Lighthouse International, 111 East 59th Street, New York, NY 10022 (E-mail: csussman@lighthouse.org).

[Haworth co-indexing entry note]: "Vision and Older Adults." Sussman-Skalka, Carol. Co-published simultaneously in *Journal of Gay & Lesbian Social Services* (Harrington Park Press, an imprint of The Haworth Press, Inc.) Vol. 13, No. 4, 2001, pp. 95-101; and: *Midlife and Aging in Gay America* (ed: Douglas C. Kimmel, and Dawn Lundy Martin) Harrington Park Press, an imprint of The Haworth Press, Inc., 2001, pp. 95-101. Single or multiple copies of this article are available for a fee from The Haworth Document Delivery Service [1-800-HAWORTH, 9:00 a.m. - 5:00 p.m. (EST). E-mail address: getinfo@haworthpressinc.com].

KEYWORDS. Vision, vision loss, sexual orientation, vision rehabilitation, vision services and resources, quality of life, older adults

VISION AND OLDER ADULTS

Adults often accept vision changes as an inevitable part of aging and assume that nothing can be done. Consequently, they do not seek help. As people age, some changes in vision are normal and can usually be corrected with a new eyeglass prescription, or in some cases, cataract surgery. But, there are vision changes caused by eye disorders, which cannot be corrected with medicine, surgery or eyeglasses. In these situations, people may find out that they have permanently impaired or low vision. Low vision does not mean complete vision loss. The term refers to a range of vision capabilities from near-normal to profound vision loss. Since the likelihood of vision impairment increases with age, all older people regardless of socio-economic status, ethnicity, race, or sexual identity need to be informed about prevention and rehabilitation. Although help is available, older adults as well as their health and human service providers are often unaware of what these services are, how they benefit people, and where to access them. Vision rehabilitation programs can make a difference by reducing unnecessary functional disability and enhancing a person's quality of life.

Vision Impairment: A Public Health Issue

According to the "Lighthouse National Survey on Vision Loss" conducted for The Lighthouse, Inc. by Louis Harris and Associates, Inc., there are compelling data to support the need for aggressive education and outreach to older adults and their service providers (The Lighthouse, 1995). One in six Americans, age 45 and older, reports some problem with their vision and the percentage rises dramatically to one in four for people age 75 and older. Only 43% of the respondents correctly recognized the following statement as a false one: "all older people will become visually impaired as a result of the normal aging process." Too many older people accept vision loss as an expected part of getting older. In addition, 42% of those people who reported a severe vision impairment–people who most needed services–were unaware of the availability of vision rehabilitation.

EDUCATING SERVICE PROVIDERS

Health and social service providers need to be informed about age-related vision impairment and the range of vision rehabilitation programs that can make a difference. With this knowledge, they are in a better position to encourage and refer older adults for appropriate services.

Lighthouse International has published *The VisualEyes™ Curriculum,* which is designed to train service providers in the aging network (Stuen, 1996). The curriculum includes information on normal changes in vision as people age and also describes functional vision impairments caused by eye diseases. Vision simulators, which approximate different types of vision loss, give participants first hand experience on the impact of different eye conditions and their affect on a person's ability to perform everyday activities. There is also a section on behavioral cues that may indicate when someone is having problems with their vision. For example, some behaviors to be aware of include lack of eye contact, inability to recognize familiar objects, bumping into things, or withdrawal from activities. A more formal tool is "The Functional Vision Screening Questionnaire" (Horowitz,1998). This questionnaire has 15 items which can be administered by an interviewer or filled out by the older person. It is easy to score and assists in identifying older people who may have a vision problem and who are in need of an optometric or ophthalmologic eye examination.

Empowering Older Adults

Equally important is reaching out to older adults in their communities and empowering them with knowledge and resources. Lighthouse International's Project InSights is a model vision education outreach program that utilizes trained older adult volunteers to educate their peers about age-related eye conditions, the importance of regular eye examinations, and the vision rehabilitation services that can help (Consorte, Offner, & Stuen, 1995). These free vision education presentations take place at community settings and reach a diverse (racial, ethnic, sexual orientation, religious) older population in the comfort of their own environment. Many of the InSights volunteers are visually impaired themselves and provide compelling testimony to how specialized training has made a difference in their quality of life. At community presentations, volunteers have discovered many people who are fearful of acknowledging a vision problem. Other issues such as an individual's cultural values, sexual preference, or race may also compound the stigma associated with vision loss. For example, many older gay and lesbian people may be hesitant to access services because they are concerned about disclosing that they are in same-sex relationships and may not feel comfortable allowing service providers into their home (Altman, 1999). The InSights volunteers who are visually impaired provide an important link by demonstrating the caring, support, and understanding they have experienced when receiving rehabilitation services.

In the mid-1980s, Lighthouse International took a leadership role in reaching out to, and collaborating with, organizations serving the gay community in order to encourage referrals for people with AIDS-related vision loss. Lighthouse educated their staff about the benefits of vision rehabilitation, and in turn became more attuned to the special issues of their clients. Lighthouse also conducted workshops at state, regional, and national conferences about service delivery issues for people with AIDS-related vision loss and published a book, *AIDS, Blindness and Low Vision,* to facilitate replication at other vision rehabilitation agencies across the country.

How Vision Rehabilitation Can Help

Vision rehabilitation helps people with vision loss learn or relearn skills. They include a variety of services, including but not limited to low vision care, rehabilitation teaching, orientation and mobility, and counseling. These services help people learn to cope with vision loss and to develop skills to continue working, managing their homes, taking care of personal needs, and participating in hobbies and other leisure activities (Sussman-Skalka, 1995). A common myth is that these services are only for the "blind." Nothing can be further from the truth. Vision rehabilitation professionals work with people with a range of vision capabilities and help them set meaningful and achievable goals based on their needs and lifestyle. Motivation is key as people take an active role in their training and regain control of their lives.

Low Vision Care

People with partial sight can benefit from a low vision evaluation performed by a specially trained ophthalmologist or optometrist. This specialized examination determines the type and severity of the individual's functional vision loss (Stuen, 1996). Once the person's vision is evaluated, optical and adaptive devices can be prescribed to help the individual perform specific tasks. While these devices do not restore normal vision, they maximize a person's remaining vision so that they may carry out many everyday tasks as well as continue leisure activities. People may need several optical devices depending on the activities they wish to do. Training and practice are essential in order to learn to use them correctly and successfully.

REHABILITATION TEACHING

Vision rehabilitation professionals also teach people skills and techniques to handle household responsibilities, personal care, communication, and recreational activities (Paskin & Soucy-Moloney, 1994). Individuals learn to use all their senses to get information about their surroundings. For example, use of color contrast can enhance the visibility of everyday objects: placing white dinner plates on dark place mats or using a bold-tip pen for writing letters assists in facilitating identification. There are also strategies that can help a person organize and identify clothing, food items, and medications. Tactile markings facilitate identification of things through the sense of touch. Since many older adults who are visually impaired do have some usable vision, use of colored or large-print labels may be preferable. Frequently used settings of ovens, dishwashers and microwaves can be marked to facilitate independent use of these appliances. People are encouraged to find a place for everything and return things to their place. There are also many adaptive devices like large print or talking watches, needle threaders, and large button phones which make life easier. Also, the use of flexible task lighting is particularly important for people with partial sight.

Orientation and Mobility

People with vision loss need to develop an awareness of themselves in relation to their surroundings while learning how to travel safely through their environment. People learn to orient themselves in space through the use of touch, sound, and their remaining vision. When orienting someone to their surroundings, it is important to describe the setting as completely as possible including the location of objects (Stuen, 1996).

There are several mobility techniques including the use of: sighted guides, long white canes, and guide dogs. With the sighted guide technique, the person with the vision impairment places their hand above the elbow of the sighted guide and walks one-half step behind. It is helpful for the sighted guide to also communicate when approaching doors or steps. Learning to use a white cane or guide dog requires special training by an orientation and mobility specialist.

Counseling

The psychological and social impact of vision loss is often devastating. People may experience a range of feelings–anger, sadness, frustration, embarrassment as well as fears of loss of control, independence, and privacy. Individual or group counseling by a professional can be beneficial. Peer support groups, often member led, are another valuable resource. Support groups provide a safe place for people to share feelings and experiences, exchange ideas and develop solutions to everyday issues (Sussman-Skalka, 1995). There is a common bond among people who are "in the same boat" dealing with similar problems and family situations. *Sharing Solutions* is a free newsletter published twice a year by Lighthouse International that provides individuals and groups nationwide with resources, information, discussion topics for support group meetings, and practical tips to cope with vision loss.

Family members and friends can play a critical and supportive role during the adjustment and relearning process. Spouses and partners in particular are adversely affected when their partner becomes visually impaired. Counseling often positively impacts relationship issues resulting from the stress associated with the functional impact of vision loss (Stuen, 1999). Gay and lesbian couples may be reluctant to reveal their sexual identity and may need to be encouraged by service providers who are sensitive and accepting (Altman, 1999).

Benefits of Vision Rehabilitation

Older adults who have received vision rehabilitation services often find themselves doing things they never thought possible. Their successes are the most compelling evidence of how vision rehabilitation helps promote independence and enhanced quality of life. As described earlier, many of the Lighthouse InSights volunteers are visually impaired and conduct vision education programs for their peers in the community (Consorte, Offner, & Stuen, 1995). As part of the program, they share their own experiences and demonstrate how their optical and adaptive devices help them continue to be productive members of society. They are especially effective advocates who often inspire others to seek help.

One visually impaired support group leader sums it up well. She said, "Training has turned our lives around. And sharing our accomplishments in our support group encourages positive attitudes" ("Coast to Coast," 2000).

REFERENCES

Altman, C. (1999). Gay and lesbian seniors: Unique challenges of coming out in later life. *Siecus Report, 22,* (3) 14-17.

Coast to coast (2000). Readers share their accomplishments. *Sharing Solutions,* 4-5.

Consorte, L., Offner, R., & Stuen, C. (1995). *The inSights manual: Vision education for older adults.* New York: The Lighthouse Inc.

Horowitz, A. (1998). Validation of a functional vision screening questionnaire for older people. In *Vision '96: Proceedings of the International Low Vision Conference, Book II* (pp. 492-494). Spain: Organización Nacional de los Ciegos de España.

Lighthouse Inc., The (1995). *The Lighthouse national survey on vision loss: The experience, attitude and knowledge of middle-aged and older Americans.* New York: Arlene R. Gordon Research Institute, The Lighthouse Inc.

Paskin, N., & Soucy-Moloney, L. A. (1994). *Whatever works.* New York: The Lighthouse Inc.

Stuen, C. (1996). Principal Investigator. *Aging and vision: The VisualEyes™ curriculum.* New York: The Lighthouse Inc.

Stuen, C. (1999). *Family involvement: Maximizing rehabilitation outcomes for older adults with a disability.* New York: Lighthouse International.

Sussman-Skalka, C. (1995). *See for yourself presenter's guidebook.* New York: The Lighthouse Inc.

Responding to the Mental Health and Grief Concerns of Homeless HIV-Infected Gay Men

Doneley Meris

SUMMARY. Aging, homeless HIV-infected gay men confront multiple bereavement and mental health issues. Needs assessment interviews with this population in the streets of New York City facilitate the initial review and provision of clinically and culturally appropriate service delivery strategies for these disenfranchised gay men to access bereavement support and mental health care systems. *[Article copies available for a fee from The Haworth Document Delivery Service: 1-800-HAWORTH. E-mail address: <getinfo@haworthpressinc.com> Website: <http://www.HaworthPress.com> © 2001 by The Haworth Press, Inc. All rights reserved.]*

KEYWORDS. Aging, HIV-positive, gay, bereavement, mental health, needs assessment, New York City, disenfranchisement, support

---

Doneley Meris, MA, a bereavement therapist in private practice, is Director of CenterBridge Bereavement Services Program of the New York City Lesbian and Gay Community Services Center and Founder and Executive Director of HIV Arts Network.

Correspondence concerning this article should be addressed to: Doneley Meris, CenterBridge Bereavement Services, Lesbian and Gay Community Services Center, One Little West 12th Street, New York, NY 10014 (E-mail: doneley@gaycenter.org).

[Haworth co-indexing entry note]: "Responding to the Mental Health and Grief Concerns of Homeless HIV-Infected Gay Men." Meris, Doneley. Co-published simultaneously in *Journal of Gay & Lesbian Social Services* (Harrington Park Press, an imprint of The Haworth Press, Inc.) Vol. 13, No. 4, 2001, pp. 103-111; and: *Midlife and Aging in Gay America* (ed: Douglas C. Kimmel, and Dawn Lundy Martin) Harrington Park Press, an imprint of The Haworth Press, Inc., 2001, pp. 103-111. Single or multiple copies of this article are available for a fee from The Haworth Document Delivery Service [1-800-HAWORTH, 9:00 a.m. - 5:00 p.m. (EST). E-mail address: getinfo@haworthpressinc.com].

Aging, homeless HIV-infected gay men have been abandoned by a society blinded with fear, ageism, homophobia, and prejudice. They are left to confront their emaciating progression with HIV/AIDS and fend for themselves as they witness other homeless persons ravaged by HIV/AIDS, tuberculosis, concurrent violence and multiple deaths. Their ever-changing and shifting living conditions cannot be separated from the impact of their HIV-related losses.

These gay men's bereavement experiences heighten their demoralization, traumatic stress, engagement in barebacking (anal sexual intercourse without a condom), and other unprotected sexual acts, alcohol and substance use, and suicidal imaginings. The personal tales of seven homeless HIV-infected gay men in the meat-packing district of New York City gallantly account for these experiences and expound on societal lack of provision and compassion for their bereavement, social services, and mental health needs.

Research focused on the living conditions, lack of social and residential services, HIV-prevention and outreach, and mental health concerns of homeless adults and youth continues to inform programming and service priorities (Allen et al., 1994; Bangsberg, Tulsky, Hecht, & Moss, 1997; Clatts, David, Sotheran, & Atillasoy, 1998; Dozier, 1991; Empfield et al., 1993; Goldfinger, Suser, Roche, & Berkman, 1998). However, comparable studies directed specifically to identify the needs of gay, lesbian, bisexual, and transgender HIV-positive and homeless persons are virtually non-existent. This pilot study will begin to shed light on the unique and difficult existence of older and HIV-positive gay men who live on the streets of America.

METHOD AND FINDINGS

Participants were recruited for this pilot program on the streets of New York City's meat-packing district, where in the late afternoons and evenings this seedy neighborhood becomes an enclave for restaurant goers, sex workers, transvestites, and the homeless. In a period of two weeks in the early spring of 2000, gay men were approached on the streets, told of the nature of the one-time interview and were invited for lunch in a nearby restaurant where the interviews took place. The open-ended questions, adapted from an intake assessment tool used in a lesbian, gay, bisexual, transgender (LGBT) mental health agency, required participants to expound on: their homelessness experiences; the chronology of their HIV illness; family and social support networks;

education; their substance use/abuse; sexuality; psychosocial and psychiatric hospitalization; and financial histories. Participants provided details about their entire social, vocational, and financial profiles prior to their time of being homeless.

The seven gay men who participated in this initial investigation met the major criteria of the study: age 50 and over, HIV-infected (based on self-report/voluntary self-disclosure), same-sex sexual engagement only, and current homeless status. The participants ranged in age from 52 to 71 years, with a mean age of 59. They came from diverse ethnic backgrounds that included two Caucasians, four African Americans, and one Puerto Rican American. The average period of homelessness was 1.46 years. Subjects have been living with the HIV virus from 2 years to 14 years, with an average of 6.82 years. All of these men completed high school. Two had some college credits but dropped out to work full time. Four of these men came to New York City from other parts of the country. Three are native New Yorkers.

Financial histories of these men reveal that they have all maintained stable careers ranging from sales, cargo-shipment, advertising, carpentry, construction, and food service. Five of these men succumbed to substance abuse (mainly cocaine and crack) that resulted in their financial devastation and familial-social abandonment. Two of the African-American men left their families in the South and opted to live on the streets, occasionally working part time. Three were eligible for government assistance but routinely utilized their monies for drugs and alcohol.

Grief Concerns

The unique psychological stresses related to an HIV/AIDS diagnosis and the premature deaths of many young adults cause existential crisis, anxiety and depression (Flaskerud, 1992; McGaffic & Longman, 1993). Societal stigmatization of gay men living with HIV/AIDS who are homeless with multiple losses due to AIDS-related deaths prove to be overwhelming and can contribute to the dysfunctional engagement with the mainstream (Carmack, 1992).

These subjects reported multiple losses prior to and during their homeless experiences. They have all seen family members and friends die from HIV/AIDS. They recalled a range of 7 to 31 HIV/AIDS-related deaths, with an average of 15 deaths. They also witnessed other deaths including those from murder, tuberculosis, lung cancer, prostate cancer, heart attack, pneumonia, gay bashing, and diabetes. They reported an average of nine such deaths during their periods of homelessness. The deceased individuals were their confidants, brothers and friends. They shared nights in subway stations, parks, and street sidewalks, stood in soup lines; weathered through winters and rainy days; helped each other to emergency rooms for urgent medical care; and witnessed the harsh realities of homophobia, crack-drug infestations and malnutrition together. In this way, the men who are the subjects of this study formed street families. These deaths devastatingly wiped out their social support networks, leaving them to cope with their multiple bereavement concerns in isolation.

All of the seven participants acknowledged that most of the HIV/AIDS-related losses and other deaths were not socially defined as significant. Hence, their disenfranchised grief requires closer scrutiny (Doka, 1989). Given their situations, these bereaved subjects are socially defined as incapable of grief, socially unrecognized for their sense of loss and periods of mourning. Their mounting losses and extraordinary living arrangements considerably factor into their developing complicated mourning (Rando, 1992). Their frequent exposure to AIDS-related deaths, their own varying physical, emotional and mental stress, living with the HIV/AIDS disease, and their own death anxieties impact on their difficult daily lives (Hintze, Templer, Cappelletty & Frederick, 1993; Templer & Greer, 1996).

One participant shared that the one time he accessed a mental health clinic and revealed his grief concerns, the focus of the social worker's intervention was on his alcohol abuse. The clinician did not acknowledge and address his bereavement issues. Such disenfranchising circumstances can further intensify these men's feelings of anger, guilt, self-destruction, powerlessness, and helplessness (Geis, Fuller & Rush, 1986; Kelly, 1977). Furthermore, the constructs of long-term adjustment to bereavement remove these men from normative grief process (Heyman & Gianturco, 1973). They carry with them the stigma, social shunning, and ostracism that inhibit them from seeking and receiving social and bereavement-mental health support (Mallinson, 1999; Schwartzberg, 1996).

The intensity of the multiple HIV/AIDS-related losses of these aging gay men complimented the findings of Cherney and Verhey (1996), identifying similar components of grief experiences. Predominant among them were the anger and hostility participants felt towards an unjust society, the lack of concrete social and mental health services specifically targeting older HIV-positive homeless gay men, the cumbersome and insensitive bureaucracy in most service institutions, and the unspoken but known prejudice towards their being gay men.

Mental Health Concerns

Equally not addressed are the mental health concerns of these older gay men. These concerns included a wide range of mental health problems: acute depression, attention deficit disorders, hallucinations, paranoia, uncontrollable rage, and their sabotaged ties with remaining family and social networks. In their fear of the prospect of being confined in what they perceive as unacceptable mental health facilities throughout the city, they choose instead to sleep on grates, subway trains and platforms, and alleyways, electing to co-habitate with the city's larger homeless population.

All of the participants reported periods of depression during their time on the streets. None of the seven men was ever medically treated for his bouts with severe depression. Two of the seven men reported having had psychiatric hospitalizations prior to living on the streets. Both stated that their hospital stay was for almost three months and that they were diagnosed with acute depression and medicated while in the psychiatric unit, but stopped taking medication after being released.

One of the participants confided that he had obsessive-compulsive tendencies (hand washing) that continued during his homeless experience. During the interview, he went twice to the restroom of the restaurant where the session was conducted. He reported having been jailed several times because of this behavior, going into offices, university facilities, and public restrooms to repeatedly wash his hands.

Another participant's behavior necessitated several pauses during the interview process. He displayed both catatonic and melancholic symptoms that prolonged the questioning and required many silent and re-framing periods.

Other Health Concerns

All of these older gay men have had to live with various sexually transmitted diseases (STDs). One of them stated that he had never been treated for such STDs. Five participants reported that to get by, they often prostituted themselves and engaged in barebacking practices in these sexual-financial transactions. This high-risk sexual behavior can have devastating effects on the health of other homeless, HIV-negative heterosexual and gay men.

Visible in two of the participants were dermatological ailments. Two participants reported ear and eye concerns that have not been medically treated. Five of the men revealed that they had high blood pressure and heart conditions that they knew required attention but had not sought help. All participants also complained about dental problems but have not accessed dental care.

Though these men rarely spent days without food, they reported malnutrition as a concern. Their resourcefulness in going to soup kitchens and meal centers throughout the city allows them at least two meals daily. However, they do not often receive balanced diets. Their HIV-positive status requires constant and specific nutritional requirements. Yet, these men have no control over their nutrition. This nutritional necessity for health combined with a loss of nutritional control makes for a serious service priority.

Prevalence of alcoholism and other substance use and abuse dominate these participants existence. All reported having at least two beers or some wine daily; they smoked cigarettes; and, they also smoked marijuana whenever they could obtain it. All used crack, cocaine, and other street drugs. They proclaimed and reaffirmed that drugs are part of the homeless culture.

The social isolation of these gay men is characterized by their withdrawal from any responsibility or any meaningful social contacts. Four out of the seven participants stated that they are better off on the streets. They feared and resented the verbal and sometimes physical assaults they experienced from care professionals in social service or mental health facilities during the brief periods when they did access service delivery institutions for emergency assistance. The despair and pessimistic outlook with the world and humans in general is intensified with such experiences. All of the participants preferred living on the streets, where they felt safer and less provoked by violence and ridicule, to the shelter system of New York City.

LIMITATIONS

With only seven subjects in this pilot study, it is not representative of the aging HIV-infected homeless gay male population. Thus, this initial investigation can not generalize its findings into this subgroup of the homeless. Although this small sample did focus on the experiences of mostly gay men of color (five out of seven), similar studies must be conducted that will target a larger sample of persons of color. Another pilot program is now underway by this investigator to examine the bereavement, mental health, and other health service needs of homeless HIV-positive Caucasian gay men. This will offer a better understanding of this percentage of the general homeless population.

Follow-up interviews with these initial seven participants, if contact can be maintained, will provide more relevant information. Outreach efforts may result in their access to current service delivery systems. In addition, the ethnicity of this investigator (Hawaiian-Filipino-American) might be a factor in the outreach and disclosure of these men. A person with a different ethnic background could generate different outcomes.

Replicating this pilot study in other urban and rural parts of the country will further identify the similar and different bereavement and health concerns of this target population.

IMPLICATIONS FOR PRACTICE AND RESEARCH

In identifying the existence of this disenfranchised group of aging gay men and acknowledging the multiplicity of their bereavement, mental health and case management needs, clinicians, homeless advocates and mental health providers can begin discussions to incorporate them in an inclusive health care delivery system. The plight of this population is an important public health problem (Allen et al., 1994; Davis, King, Sawyer, Warn & MacDonald, 1990). Their HIV/AIDS treatment, mental health, and housing priorities should be integrated into comprehensive health and medical programs.

The use of chronological age as a determinant for service eligibility and reconfiguration of funding streams will put the health needs and bereavement concerns of these gay men on the map of health care planning (Clatts, Davis, Sotheran, & Atillasoy, 1998). In addition, mental health practitioners must be encouraged to work more closely with the clergy and together recognize the depression and suicide potential of homeless HIV-positive gay men (McIntosh, 1988; Weaver & Koenig, 1996). By collaboratively discovering and implementing effective street outreach, social-housing services, and pastoral care programs to this population (Moore, 1997), better screening suicide lethality strategies can be utilized to assist them (Pieper & Garrison, 1992). It is equally important that culturally appropriate (homosexual and homeless-sensitive) outreach strategies be developed so these men can begin to access mental health and grief care systems and proactively experience a better quality of life.

In identifying funding streams to further investigate service, housing and mental health needs of these men, health advocates can address the service requirements and the integration of these men into present support systems. It is the responsibility and humane commitment of both the lesbian, gay, bisexual, and transgender service delivery professionals and general professionals to meet the needs of these forgotten individuals.

REFERENCES

Allen, D. M., Lehman, J. S., Green, T. A., Lindegren, M. L., Onarato, I. M., & Forrester, W. (1994). HIV infection among homeless adults and runaway youth, United States, 1989-1992, Field Services Branch. *AIDS, 8*, 1593-1598.

Bangsberg, D., Tulsky, J. P., Hecht, F. M., & Moss, A. R. (1997). Protease inhibitors in the homeless. *Journal of the American Medical Association, 278*(1), 63-65.

Carmack, B. (1992). Balancing engagement/detachment in AIDS-related multiple losses. *Image: The Journal of Nursing Scholarship, 24*(1), 9-14.

Cherney, P. M., & Verhey, M. P. (1996). Grief among gay men associated with multiple losses from AIDS. *Death Studies, 20*, 115-132.

Clatts, M.C., Davis, W. R., Sotheran, J. L., & Atillasoy, A. (1998). Correlates and distribution of HIV risk behaviors among homeless youths in New York City: Implications for prevention and policy. *Child Welfare, 77*(2), 195-207.

Davis, J. L., King, C., Sawyer, E., Warn, D., & Macdonald, K. (1990). Housing and residential health-related facilities for people with AIDS. *International Conference on AIDS, 6*:469 (abstract #: 4060).

Doka, K. (1989). *Disenfranchised grief: Recognizing hidden sorrow.* New York: Lexington Books.

Dozier, C. E. (1991). Perception of risk for HIV infection: AIDS among homeless veterans in New York City shelters. *International Conference on AIDS, 7*:393 (Abstract #: W.D. 4023.

Empfield, M., Cournos, F., Meyer, I., McKinnon, K., Horwath, E., Silver, M., & Schrage. H. (1993). HIV seroprevalence among homeless patients admitted to a psychiatric inpatient unit. *American Journal of Psychiatry, 150*: 47-52.

Flaskerud, J. (1992). Psychosocial aspects. In J. Flaskerud & P. Ungvarski (Eds.), *HIV/AIDS: Guide to nursing care* (2nd ed., pp. 230-274). Philadelphia: Saunders.

Geis, S., Fuller, R., & Rush, J. (1986). Lovers of AIDS victims: Psychosocial stresses and counseling needs. *Death Studies, 10*, 43-54.

Goldfinger, S. M., Susser, E., Roche, B. A., & Berkman, A. (1998). *HIV, homelessness and serious mental illness: Implications for policy and practice.* Rockville, MD: Center for Mental Health Services.

Heyman, D., & Gianturco, D. (1973). Long-term adaptation by the elderly in bereavement. *Journal of Gerontology, 28*, 359-362.

Hintze, J., Templer, D. I., Cappelletty, G., & Frederick, W. (1993). Death depression and death anxiety in HIV-infected males. *Death Studies, 17,* 333-341.

Kelly, J. (1977). The aging male homosexual: Myth and reality. *The Gerontologist, 17,* 328-332.

Mallinson, R. K. (1999). The lived experience of AIDS-related multiple losses by HIV-negative gay men. *Journal of the Association of Nurses in AIDS Care, 10*(5), 22-31.

McGaffic, C. M., & Longman, A. J. (1993). Connecting and disconnecting: Bereavement experiences of six gay men. *Journal of the Association of Nurses in AIDS Care, 4*(1), 49-57.

McIntosh, J. L. (1988). Suicide: Training and education needs with an emphasis on the elderly. *Gerontology & Geriatrics Education, 7*(3/4), 125-139.

Moore, P. J. (1997). Providing bereavement services to African Americans: Role of the black church in implementing social welfare reform. In A. Rodgers (Ed.), *Social welfare reform: New realities and new strategies for the twenty-first century.* Columbia, SC: College of Social Work, University of South Carolina.

Pieper, H. G., & Garrison, T. (1992). Knowledge of social aspects of aging among pastors. *Journal of Religious Gerontology, 8*(4), 89-105.

Rando, T. A. (1992). The increasing prevalence of complicated mourning: The onslaught is just beginning. *OMEGA, 26,* 43-59.

Schwartzberg, S. S. (1996). *The crisis in meaning: How gay men are making sense of AIDS.* New York: Oxford University Press.

Templer, D. I., & Greer, R. C. D. (1996). Death anxiety and HIV disease. *Focus, 11*(2) 1-4.

Weaver, A. J., & Koenig, H. G. (1996). Elderly suicide, mental health professionals, and the clergy: A need for clinical collaboration, training and research. *Death Studies,* 20:495-508.

Index